N I X O N

An Oliver Stone Film

D1077966

NIXON

An Oliver Stone Film

EDITED BY ERIC HAMBURG

INCLUDES THE ORIGINAL SCREENPLAY BY STEPHEN J.
RIVELE, CHRISTOPHER WILKINSON, AND OLIVER STONE

BLOOMSBURY

First published in Great Britain 1996
Bloomsbury Publishing Plc,
2 Soho Square, London W1V 6HB

Copyright © 1995, Cinergi Productions, Inc.

Cover photo by Sidney Baldwin,
Copyright © 1995 Track 2 Productions, Inc

The moral right of the author has been asserted

A CIP catalogue record for this book
is available from the British Library

ISBN 0 7475 2726 1

10 9 8 7 6 5 4 3 2 1

Printed in Great Britain by
Caledonian International Book Manufacturing

It is not the critic who counts; not the man who points out how the strong man stumbles, or where the doer of deeds could have done them better. The credit belongs to the man who is actually in the arena, whose face is marred by dust and sweat and blood; who strives valiantly; who errs, and comes short again and again; because there is not effort without error and shortcoming; but who does actually strive to do the deeds; who knows the enthusiasms, the great devotions; who spends himself in a worthy cause, who at the best knows in the end the triumphs of high achievement and who at the worst, if he fails, at least fails while daring greatly, so that his place shall never be with those cold and timid souls who know neither victory nor defeat.

—THEODORE ROOSEVELT
as quoted by Richard Nixon

Cast List

RICHARD NIXON	*Anthony Hopkins*
PAT NIXON	*Joan Allen*
H. R. HALDEMAN	*James Woods*
JOHN EHRLICHMAN	*J. T. Walsh*
HENRY KISSINGER	*Paul Sorvino*
ALEXANDER HAIG	*Powers Boothe*
JOHN DEAN	*David Hyde Pierce*
JOHN MITCHELL	*E. G. Marshall*
MARTHA MITCHELL	*Madeline Kahn*
RON ZIEGLER	*David Paymer*
HERB KLEIN	*Saul Rubineck*
CHUCK COLSON	*Kevin Dunn*
MANOLO SANCHEZ	*Tony Plana*
J. EDGAR HOOVER	*Bob Hoskins*
MURRAY CHOTINER	*Fyvush Finkel*
JOHNNY ROSELLI	*Tomy Lo Bianco*
GORDON LIDDY	*John Diehl*
HOWARD HUNT	*Ed Harris*
FRANK STURGIS	*Robert Beltran*
BILL ROGERS	*James Karen*
MEL LAIRD	*Richard Fancy*
JULIE NIXON	*Annabeth Gish*
TRICIA NIXON	*Marley Shelton*
FRANK NIXON	*Tom Bower*
HANNAH NIXON	*Mary Steenbergen*
RICHARD NIXON @12	*Corey Carrier*
RICHARD NIXON @19	*David Barry Gray*
DONALD NIXON	*Sean Stone*
ARTHUR NIXON	*Joshua Preston*
HAROLD NIXON @16	*Tony Goldwyn*

HAROLD NIXON @23	*Tony Goldwyn*
JACK JONES	*Larry Hagman*
TRINI CARDOZA	*Dan Hedaya*
CUBAN MAN	*John Bedford Lloyd*
MITCH	*O'Neal Compton*
FAN #1	*Harry Murphy*
FAN #2	*Suzanne Schnulle Murphy*
SANDY	*Bridgitte Wilson*
CONVENTION ANNOUNCER	*Mike Kennedy*
TERESA	*Pamela Dickerson*
CLYDE TOLSON	*Brian Bedford*
JOAQUIN	*Wilson Cruz*
VERNON WALTERS	*Roy Barnitt*
RICHARD HELMS	*Sam Waterston*
LEONID BREZHNEV	*Boris Sichkin*
ANDREI GROMYKO	*Fima Noveck*
RUSSIAN INTERPRETER	*Raissa Danilova*
JAMES MCCORD	*Ron Von Klaussen*
FRED BUZHARDT	*George Plimpton*
NELSON ROCKEFELLER	*Ed Herrmann*
MAO TSE-TUNG	*Ric Young*
CHINESE INTERPRETER	*Bai Ling*
BETHESDA DOCTOR	*Bill Bolender*
FLOOR MANAGER	*Michael Kaufman*
JFK DOUBLE	*James Kelly*
PROTESTER #1	*Wass Stevens*
REPORTER #1	*John Tenney*
REPORTER #2	*Julie Araskog*
REPORTER #3	*Ray Wills*
REPORTER #4	*John Bellucci*
REPORTER #5	*Zoey Zimmerman*

STAFFER #1	John Stockwell
STAFFER #2	Charlie Haugk
STUDENT #1	Breck Wilson
STUDENT #2	Peter Carlin
YOUNG WOMAN	Joanna Going
BLACK ORATOR	James Pickens
WHITE HOUSE SECURITY	Mark Steines
COCK HANDLER #1	Humberto Martinez
SECRET SERVICE AGENT	Tom Nicoletti
SECRET SERVICE AGENT	Chuck Pfeiffer
WEDDING GUEST	Phyllis Samhaber
KISSINGER DATE	Nicole Nagle
STUDIO AUDIENCE #1	Diane Armbuster
GREETER	Jesus Cabildo
BULL RIDER	Scott Giliis
HAPPY ROCKEFELLER	Annette Helde
PARTY GUEST #1	Paul Boyle
PARTY GUEST #2	Jaxon Redding
RINGMASTER	Albert Leon
CUBAN PLUMBER	Lenny Vullo
FOOTBALL COACH	Jack Wallace
ASST. COACH	James Raskin
FOOTBALL PLAYER	Ian Calip
BOB	John Cunningham
MAUREEN DEAN	Donna Dixon
WOMAN STAFFER #1	Jenne Lee
STUDENT #4	Michelle Matheson
ROSEMARY WOODS	Mary Rudolph
SPIRO AGNEW	Bob Marshall
YOUNG PAT NIXON	Julie Condra Douglas
EARL	John C. McGinley
VIRGILIO GONZALES	Enrique Castillo

NIXON

Editor's Note: *This is the shooting script used in filming Nixon. Inevitably, during the course of filming, changes were made when the director or actors found it necessary to modify lines. Also, scenes are sometimes shot out of chronological order, and only during the final editing process is the determination made as to how the footage plays best. Finally, the editing process itself results in changes, as the director seeks to arrange and present the material in a manner that meets his creative instincts and experience as a storyteller. Thus, this annotated script may vary in some instances from the film.*

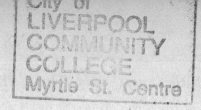
PROLOGUE

A PROLOGUE APPEARS on black screen:
This film is an attempt to understand the truth of
Richard Nixon, thirty-seventh President of the United
States. It is based on numerous public sources and on an
incomplete historical record.

   In consideration of length, events and characters have
been condensed, and some scenes among protagonists
have been conjectured.

   On a portable screen we read the famous words from
Matthew: 'What shall it profit a man if he shall gain
the whole world and lose his own soul?' This FADES
into:

   A BLACK AND WHITE 16-mm sales training FILM.
At the moment, the sales manager, BOB, is chatting with
EARL, a rookie salesman.

BOB: Sure you've got a great product, Earl. But you have
   to remember what you're really selling. *(then)*
   Yourself.

1. INT. WATERGATE HOTEL. CONFERENCE ROOM. NIGHT.
Seven men in shirts and ties are seated around a table in
the darkened room. They are smoking Cuban cigars, idly
watching the film.

3

TITLE: 'JUNE 17, 1972.' Then: 'THE WATERGATE HOTEL'

A BUSBOY yawns as he clears away the remains of dinner. A WAITER starts pouring Margaritas from a pitcher.

A balding man in his early fifties tosses a five onto the table. He is HOWARD HUNT.

HUNT: Just leave it.
  The waiter puts down the pitcher, picks up the five, and follows the busboy out of the room.
  The moment the door closes behind them, GORDON LIDDY is on his feet, locking the door. OTHER MEN are visible, putting on jackets, securing technical equipment from briefcases and bags. They are: FRANK STURGIS, BERNARD BARKER, EUGENIO MARTINEZ, VIRGILIO GONZALES, and JAMES McCORD.

LIDDY (checks his watch): Zero-one-twenty-one. Mark.
  Sturgis rolls his eyes, drains his Margarita. Liddy pulls a wad of cash from his pocket, starts passing out hundred-dollar bills to his men.

LIDDY: Just in case you need to buy a cop. But don't spend it all in one place. We're going to do McGovern's office later tonight.
  McCord shakes his head.

LIDDY: Orders from the White House, partner.
  Liddy bypasses Hunt, who is browsing a folded Spanish-language paper.

4

LIDDY: Howard . . . What the hell? What're you doing?

HUNT: Dogs . . . Season starts tomorrow. (*off Liddy's look*) It keeps me calm. I don't like going back into the same building four times.
Liddy mutters something didactic in German.

HUNT: *Mein Kampf?*

LIDDY (*translates to English*): 'A warrior with nerves of steel is yet broken by a thread of silk.' Nietzsche.

HUNT: Personally I'd prefer a greyhound with a shot of speed.

LIDDY (*to all*): Remember – listen up! Fire team discipline in there at all times. Keep your radios on *at all times* during the entire penetration. Check yourselves. Phony ID's, no wallets, no keys. We rendezvous where? The Watergate, Room 214. When? At zero-three-hundred.

STURGIS: Yawohl, mein fartenfuhrer.

LIDDY (*narrowing, waving his gun*): Don't start with me, Frank, I'll make you a new asshole.

HUNT (*rising past them*): Let's get the fuck out of here, shall we ladies?

LIDDY: Anything goes wrong, head for your homes, just sit tight – you'll hear from me or Howard.

HUNT (*aside*): Personally I'll be calling the President of the United States.
A nervous chuckle as Hunt follows Liddy out the

main door. *The rest exit through the door behind the screen.*

The FILM is ending. Bob puts a hand on Earl's shoulder.

BOB: And remember, Earl: Always look 'em in the eye. *(to the camera)* Nothing sells like sincerity.

A BLACK SCREEN as the film rattles out, followed by a RADIO REPORT *over the darkened room, the sounds of doors closing.*

RADIO REPORT (V.O.): Five men wearing surgical gloves and business suits, and carrying cameras and electronic surveillance equipment, were arrested early today in the headquarters of the Democratic National Committee in Washington. They were unarmed. Nobody knows yet why they were there or what they were looking for . . .

FADE IN TO:

2. EXT. THE WHITE HOUSE. NIGHT. 1973
TITLES RUN – A raw November night. We are looking through the black iron bars of the fence towards the facade of the Executive Mansion. A LIGHT is on in a second floor room.

We move towards it through the bars, across the lawn. Dead leaves blow past. A SUBTITLE READS:
'NOVEMBER 1973'

A black LIMOUSINE slides up to the White House West Wing. An armed GUARD *with a black* DOBERMAN *approaches.*

The window opens slightly. The Guard peers in. Then, he opens the door.

GUARD: Good evening, General Haig.

GENERAL ALEXANDER HAIG *gets out, walks up the steps. He carries a manila envelope. As he enters the White House, we hear an AUDIO MONTAGE of NEWS REPORTERS from the previous year. The VOICES fade in and out, overlap:*

REPORTERS (V.O.): Judge John Sirica today sentenced the Watergate burglars to terms ranging up to forty years . . . The White House continues to deny any involvement . . .

3. INT. THE WHITE HOUSE. VESTIBULE. NIGHT.
HAIG *enters, starts up the stairs. The mansion is dark, silent. Like a tomb.*

REPORTERS (V.O.: *continues*): Presidential counsel John Dean testified before the Senate Watergate Committee that the scandal reaches to the highest levels . . .
MOVING: *A low-angle shot of Haig's spit-shined shoes moving down the long corridor of the second floor of the Residence.*

REPORTERS (V.O.: *continues*): Presidential aides Haldeman and Ehrlichman were ordered to resign today . . . In a stunning announcement, White House aide Alexander Butterfield revealed the existence of a secret taping system . . .

CLOSE: *on the manila envelope in Haig's hand.*

REPORTERS (*V.O.: continues*): The President has fired the
   Watergate Special Prosecutor, Archibald Cox,
   provoking the gravest constitutional crisis in
   American history . . .
   Haig stops at a door, quietly knocks. No answer.

REPORTERS (*V.O.: continues*): Judge Sirica has ordered
   the President to turn over his tapes . . .
   Haig opens the door.

4. INT. THE WHITE HOUSE. LINCOLN SITTING ROOM.
NIGHT.
*The room is small, austere, dominated by a portrait of
LINCOLN over the fireplace.* HAIG *stands in the
doorway, holding the envelope.*

HAIG: These are the tapes you requested, Mr. President.
   RICHARD NIXON *is in shadow, silhouetted by the fire
   in the hearth. The air-conditioning is going full blast.
   Haig crosses the room, opens the envelope, takes out
   a reel of tape.*
   *Nixon sits in a small armchair in a corner. A Uher
   tape recorder and a headset are on an end table at
   his elbow. Next to it is a large tumbler of Scotch.
   Haig hands the envelope containing the tapes to
   Nixon.*

NIXON: This is June twentieth?

HAIG: It's marked. Also there's June twenty-third. And

8

this year – March twenty-first. Those are the ones . . .
Nixon squints at the label in the firelight.

HAIG: . . . the lawyers feel . . . will be the basis of the . . .
proceedings.
Nixon tries to thread the tape.

NIXON: Nixon's never been good with these things.
He drops the tape on the floor.

NIXON: Cocksucker!
*Haig picks up the tape. Then he steps to the table,
reaches for the lamp.*

HAIG: Do you mind?
*Nixon gestures awkwardly. Haig turns on the lamp.
For the first time we can see Nixon's face: he hasn't
slept in days, dark circles, sagging jowls, five-o'clock
shadow. He hates the light, slurs a strange growl –
the effect of sleeping pills.*

HAIG: Sorry . . .

NIXON (*gestures*): . . . go on.
*Haig threads the tape. Nixon, looking at it,
remembers.*

NIXON: . . . Y'know Al, if Hoover was alive none of this
would've happened. He would've protected the
President.

HAIG: Mr. Hoover was a realist.

NIXON: I trusted Mitchell. It was that damn big mouth
wife of his.

HAIG: At least Mitchell stood up to it.

NIXON: Not like the others – Dean, McCord, the rest . . .
We never got our side of the story out, Al. People've
forgotten. I mean: 'Fuck you, Mr. President, fuck
you Tricia, fuck you Julie!' and all that shit, just
words, but what violence! The tear gassing, the riots,
burning the draft cards, Black Panthers – we fixed it,
Al, and they hate me for it – the double-dealing
bastards. They lionize that traitor, Ellsberg, for
stealing secrets, but they jump all over me 'cause it's
Nixon *(repeats)* . . . They've always hated Nixon.
Haig finishes threading.

HAIG: May I say something, Mr. President?

NIXON: There's no secrets here, Al.

HAIG: You've never been a greater example to the
country than you are now, sir, but . . . but you need
to get out more, sir, and talk to people. No one I
know feels . . . close to you.
Nixon looks at him, moved by his concern.

NIXON: I was never the buddy-buddy type, Al. You
know, 'Oh I couldn't sleep last night, I was thinking
of my mother who beat me' – all that kinda crap,
you know the psychoanalysis bag . . . My mother . . .
The more I'd spill my guts, the more they'd hate me.
I'd be what . . . *pathetic!* If I'd bugged out of
Vietnam when they wanted, do you think Watergate
would've ever happened? You think the
Establishment would've given a shit about a third-

10

rate burglary? But did I? Quit? Did I pull out? *(he stares, waits)*

HAIG: No, sir, you did not.

NIXON: Damn right. And there's still a helluva lotta people out there who wanna believe . . . That's the point, isn't it? They wanna believe in the President. *He suddenly tires of talking, rubs his hands over his face.*

HAIG: You're all set, sir. Just push this button. Good night, Mr. President.

NIXON: You know, Al, men in your profession . . . you give 'em a pistol and you leave the room. *(Haig: 'I don't have a pistol.')* 'Night, Al . . . *Haig quietly closes the door. Nixon takes a generous slug of Scotch. Then he looks down at the tape recorder. He puts on the UHER headset, and hits the 'fast forward' button: high-speed VOICES.*

NIXON: Goddamn! *He hits 'stop,' puts on his eyeglasses, studies the recorder a moment. Pushes the 'play' button. VOICES. Barely audible at first. Nixon leans closer, listening.*

NIXON *(on tape)*: They did what?! I don't understand. Why'd they go into O'Brien's office *in the first place*?

HALDEMAN *(on tape)*: Evidently to install bugs and photograph documents. *FLASHBACK TO:*

5. INT. EXECUTIVE OFFICE BLDG. PRESIDENT'S OFFICE. DAY (1972).

SUBTITLE READS: 'JUNE 1972.'

NIXON'*s hideaway office.* BOB HALDEMAN, *his crew-cut, hard-edged chief of staff, sits across the desk, a folder open on his lap. Nixon, at his desk, seems a healthier man than in the previous scene. Also there are* JOHN EHRLICHMAN, *portly domestic advisor, and* JOHN DEAN, *blond, gentrified legal counsel.*

NIXON (*cont'd*): But O'Brien doesn't even use that office. The Democrats've moved to Miami. There's nothing there!

HALDEMAN: It was just a fishing expedition. Apparently it was their fourth attempt at the DNC. (*Nixon: 'Their fourth!'*) It's possible they were looking for evidence of an illegal Howard Hughes donation to the Democrats, so the Democrats couldn't make an issue of your Hughes money.

NIXON: Contribution! It was a legal contribution. Who the hell authorized this? Colson?

EHRLICHMAN (*shakes his head*): Colson doesn't know a thing about it; he's pure as a virgin on this one. It's just not clear the burglars knew what they were looking for. They were heading to McGovern's office later that night.

NIXON: Jesus! Did Mitchell know?

EHRLICHMAN: Mitchell's out of his mind right now.

Martha just put her head through a plate-glass window.

NIXON: Jesus! Through a window?

HALDEMAN: It was her wrist. And it was through a plate-glass door.

EHRLICHMAN: Anyway, they had to take her to Bellevue. Maybe she'll stay this time.
A beat.

NIXON: Martha's an idiot, she'll do anything to get John's attention. If Mitchell'd been minding the store instead of that nut, Martha, we wouldn't have that kid Magruder runnin' some third-rate burglary! Was he smoking pot?

EHRLICHMAN: Mitchell?

NIXON: No! Magruder! That sonofabitch tests my Quaker patience to the breaking point.

DEAN: The bigger problem I see is this guy who was arrested, McCord – James McCord – he headed up security for the Committee to Re-Elect. He turns out to be ex-CIA.

NIXON: 'Ex-CIA'? There's no such thing as 'ex-CIA,' John – they're all Ivy League establishment. Is he one of these guys with a beef against us?

EHRLICHMAN: McCord? . . .

13

NIXON: Find out what the hell he was doing at 'CREEP.' This could be trouble. These CIA guys don't miss a trick. This could be a set-up.
INTERCUTS of all these people arise as the scene runs – McCord, Liddy, Magruder, Mitchell, Martha, Hunt, etc.

HALDEMAN (*with a look to Ehrlichman*): We feel the bigger concern is Gordon Liddy . . .

NIXON: That fruitcake! What about him?

HALDEMAN: Well, you know, sir, he's a nut. He used to work here with the 'Plumbers' and now he's running this Watergate caper. You remember his plan to firebomb the Brookings using Cubans as firemen? He wanted to buy a damned fire truck! Magruder thinks he's just nutty enough to go off the reservation.

NIXON: What's Liddy got?

HALDEMAN: Apparently he was using some campaign cash that was laundered for us through Mexico. The FBI's onto it. We could have a problem with that.

DEAN: . . . But it'll just be a campaign finance violation . . .

HALDEMAN: . . . And if Liddy takes the rap for Watergate, we can take care of him . . .

NIXON (*looking at his watch*): I don't have time for all this shit! (*to Haldeman*) Just handle it, Bob! Keep it out of the White House. What else? Kissinger's waiting – he's gonna throw a tantrum again if I don't see him, threatening to quit . . . again. (*sighs*)

EHRLICHMAN (*reluctant*): Well, sir . . . it turns out – one of the people implicated is still, you see, on our White House payroll.

NIXON: Who? Not another Goddamn Cuban?

HALDEMAN: No, sir. A guy named Hunt.
Nixon stops, stunned.

NIXON: Hunt? Howard Hunt?

EHRLICHMAN: He left his White House phone number in his hotel room.

HALDEMAN: He works for Colson. He used him on the Pentagon Papers. We're trying to figure out when he officially stopped being a White House consultant. After the arrest he dumped his wiretapping stuff into his White House safe.

NIXON (*incredulous*): Howard Hunt is working for the White House? No shit! This is Goddamn Disneyland! Since when?

EHRLICHMAN: Chappaquiddick. You wanted some dirt on Kennedy. Colson brought him in.

DEAN: You know Hunt, sir?

NIXON (*perturbed*): On the list of horribles, I know what he is. And I know what he tracks back to. (*then*) You say he was involved in the Plumbers?

HALDEMAN: Definitely. Colson had him trying to break into Bremer's apartment after Bremer shot Wallace, to plant McGovern campaign literature.

NIXON (*lofty*): I had nothing to do with that. Was he . . .
in the Ellsberg thing?

HALDEMAN: Yes, you approved it, sir.

NIXON: I did?

HALDEMAN: It was right after the Pentagon Papers
broke. They went in to get his psychiatric records.

NIXON: Fucking hell.

HALDEMAN: We were working on China . . .
*Nixon has taken a seat, shaken. He stares right at us
as we:*
SHARP CUT BACK TO:

6. INT. OVAL OFFICE. DAY (1971).
*The PRESIDENT'S MEN are gathered in somber silence,
sharing front page copies of the* New York Times.
SUBTITLE READS: 'JUNE 1971 – A YEAR EARLIER'
   *INSERT HEADLINE: 'Secret Pentagon Study Details
Descent into Vietnam'; 'Pentagon Papers Expose
Government Lies.'*
   *The technique we've established of an AUDIO
MONTAGE of REPORTERS' VOICES continues over
the scene.*

REPORTERS (*V.O.*): The *New York Times* began
publishing today the first in a series of *forty-seven
volumes* of top secret Pentagon Papers relating to the
war in Vietnam. The papers reveal a systematic

pattern of government lies about American
involvement in the war . . .
NIXON *throws down the paper in disgust and
attempts to feed his Irish setter, KING TIMAHOE, a
biscuit, as* HENRY KISSINGER *paces the room, the
most upset of all.*

KISSINGER: Mr. President, we are in a revolutionary
situation. We are under siege – Black Panthers,
Weathermen; the State Department under Rogers is
leaking like a sieve. And now this insignificant little
shit, Ellsberg, publishing all the diplomatic secrets of
this country, will destroy our ability to conduct
foreign policy!

NIXON (*feeding the dog*): Here, Tim . . . Tim. I'm as
frustrated as you, Henry, but don't you think this
one's a Democrat problem. They started the war; it
makes them look bad.
Kissinger lowers his voice for effect, pounds the desk.

KISSINGER: Mr. President, how can we look the Soviets
or the Chinese in the eye now and have any
credibility when any traitor can leak! Even the
Vietnamese, tawdry little shits that they are, will
never – *never* – agree to secret negotiations with us.
This makes you look like a *weakling,* Mr. President.

HALDEMAN: He's right about one thing, sir. I spoke with
Lyndon. This Pentagon Papers business has knocked
the shit out of him. Complete collapse, massive
depression. He feels the country is lost, that you as
President can't govern anymore.

17

Nixon is bent from the waist, stiffly extending the biscuit, but the dog still won't come.

NIXON (*irritated*): Goddamn! How long have we had this fucking dog?! Two years, he still doesn't come! We need a dog that looks happy when the press is around.

EHRLICHMAN: Well, he's photogenic. Let's try dog bones?

KISSINGER (*end of his patience*): Mr. President, the Vietnamese, the Russians . . .
Nixon finally throws the biscuit at the dog, glares at Kissinger.

NIXON (*to Ehrlichman*): Fuck it! He doesn't like me, John! *(to Kissinger)* It's your fault, Henry.

KISSINGER: I beg your pardon –

NIXON: It's your people who are leaking to the *Times*. Wasn't this Ellsberg a student of yours at Harvard? He was your idea; why are you suddenly running for cover?

KISSINGER: He was, he was. We taught a class together at Harvard. But you know these back-stabbing Ivy League intellectuals, they can't . . .

NIXON (*cold*): No, Henry, I don't.

KISSINGER: He's turned into a drug fiend, he shot people from helicopters in Vietnam, he has sexual relations with his wife in front of their children. He sees a shrink in L.A. He's all fucked up. Now he's trying to be a hero to the liberals . . . If he gets away with it, everybody will follow his lead. He must be stopped at all costs.

COLSON: Sir, if I might?

NIXON: Go, Chuck.

COLSON: For three years now I've watched people in this government promote themselves, ignoring your orders, embarrassing your administration. It makes me sick! We've played by the rules and it doesn't work!

MITCHELL (*to Nixon*): We can prosecute the *New York Times,* go for an injunction . . .

NIXON: . . . but it's not, bottom-line, gonna change a Goddamn thing, John. The question is: How do we screw Ellsberg so bad it puts the fear of God into all leakers?

COLSON: Can we link Ellsberg to the Russians?

NIXON: Good, I like that. The other issue is: How the hell do we plug these leaks once and for all? Who the hell's talking to the press? (*he looks directly at Henry*) Henry, for two Goddamn years you've put wiretaps on your own people.

KISSINGER: To protect you, Mr. President.

COLSON (*interjects*): To protect yourself is more like it. The pot calling the kettle . . .

Kissinger throws Colson a vicious look, while Nixon ignores it.

KISSINGER (*aside*): Who are you talking to like this, you insignificant shit . . .

NIXON: . . . and what do we get for it? Gobs and gobs of bullshit, gossip, *nothing!* Someone is leaking. We've got to stop the leaks, Henry, at any cost, do you hear me? Then we can go for the big play – China, Russia.

COLSON: Mr. President, we can do this ourselves. The CIA and the FBI aren't doing the job. But we can create our own intelligence unit – right here, inside the White House.
A slow move in on Nixon as he thinks about it.

NIXON: Well, why not?

HALDEMAN: Our own intelligence capability – to fix the leaks?

COLSON: Yeah, like plumbers.
Nixon smiles.

NIXON: I like it. I like the idea.

EHRLICHMAN: Is it legal? (*a beat*) I mean has anyone ever done it before?

NIXON: Sure. Lyndon, JFK, FDR – I mean, Truman cut the shit out of my investigation of Hiss back in '48.

MITCHELL: It was illegal, what he did.

NIXON: You know, this kinda thing, you gotta be brutal.
A leak happens, the whole damn place should be
fired. Really. You do it like the Germans in World
War II. If they went through these towns and a
sniper hit one of them, they'd line the whole
Goddamned town up and say: 'Until you talk you're
all getting shot.' I really think that's what has to be
done. I don't think you can be Mr. Nice-guy
anymore . . .

COLSON: Just whisper the word to me, sir, and I'll shoot
Ellsberg myself.

EHRLICHMAN: We're not Germans, sir . . .

NIXON: Ellsberg's not the issue. The Pentagon Papers
aren't the issue. *(almost to himself)* It's the lie.
*A pause. Everyone in the room chews on this for a
moment.* MITCHELL, *the oldest in the group, smokes
on his pipe, stone-faced.*

MITCHELL: The lie?

NIXON: You remember, John, in '48 – no one believed
Alger Hiss was a Communist. Except me. They
loved Hiss just like they love this Ellsberg character.
East Coast, Ivy League. He was their kind. I was dirt
to them. Nothing.
*As they talk, a MONTAGE arises of ALGER HISS
and the days of old – the photographs of the
notorious 1948 Hiss case: HISS, CHAMBERS, the
YOUNGER NIXON with the microfilm; a headline
reading 'HISS FOUND GUILTY'; TRUMAN,*

21

ELEANOR ROOSEVELT, a beaming
EISENHOWER shaking Nixon's hand.

MITCHELL (*to the room*): And Dick beat the shit out of them.

NIXON: But I wouldn't have if Hiss hadn't lied about knowing Chambers. The documents were old and out of date, like these Pentagon Papers. The key thing we proved was that Hiss was a liar. Then people bought that he was a spy. (*then*) It's the lie that gets you.

MITCHELL (*to the room*): Hiss was protecting his wife. I've always believed that.

NIXON (*cryptically*): When they know you've got something to protect, that's when they fuck you!

HALDEMAN: What's this faggot, Ellsberg, protecting?

COLSON: His liberal elitist friends. His Harvard-Ph.D.-I-shit-holier-than-thou attitude.
Kissinger waits. Nixon acknowledges him. The camera is moving tighter and tighter on the President. His expression is furious, his words violent.

NIXON (*cont'd*): Alright, Henry – we're gonna go your way. Crush this Ellsberg character the same way we did Hiss!

KISSINGER (*interjects*): There's no other choice.

NIXON: We're gonna hit him so hard he looks like everything that's sick and evil about the Eastern Establishment. *(to Colson)* You and your 'plumbers' are gonna find the dirt on this guy – let's see him going to the bathroom in front of the American public! And when we finish with him, they'll crucify him!
FLASH CUT TO:

7. INT. FIELDING PSYCHIATRIST OFFICE. NIGHT (1971).
SUBTITLE READS: 'ELLSBERG'S PSYCHIATRIST'S OFFICE. 1971'
ANOTHER BREAK-IN is in effect. LIDDY in wig, thick glasses, false teeth, and THREE CUBANS (Barker, Martinez from Watergate, and de Diego, not at Watergate) are visible, moving through, smashing up the office. In CLOSE-UPS, we see hands jerking open filing cabinets, pulling the drawers out of desks.

REPORTERS *(V.O. cont'd)*: The Nixon Administration responded by filing an injunction against the *New York Times* to prevent further publication . . . President Nixon condemned the Pentagon Papers as the worst breach of national security in U.S. history . . . Daniel Ellsberg, who leaked the papers, was charged today in federal court . . .
While this is going on, a powerful FLASHBULB keeps popping. The photographer, looking for evidence, suddenly catches his partner in the light, his startled face buried beneath a 70's wig –

HOWARD HUNT. Hunt is pissed: 'Fuck you –
gimme that fucking film!'
BACK TO:

8. INT. EXECUTIVE OFFICE BLDG. PRESIDENT'S OFFICE. DAY
(1972).
RESUME – CLOSE on NIXON *remembering Howard*
Hunt, as HALDEMAN *looks on.*

NIXON: Howard Hunt? . . . Jesus Christ, you open up
that scab . . . and you uncover a lot of pus.

HALDEMAN: What do you mean, sir?
Nixon chooses not to answer.

NIXON: Where's Hunt now?

EHRLICHMAN: In hiding. He sent Liddy to talk to me.

NIXON: And?

EHRLICHMAN: He wants money.

NIXON: Pay him.

EHIRLICHMAN: Pay him? I told him to get out of the
country. It's crazy to start . . .

NIXON: What the hell are you doing, Ehrlichman –
screwing with the CIA? I don't care how much he
wants – pay him.

HALDEMAN: But what are we paying him for?

NIXON: Silence!

HALDEMAN: But sir, you're covered – no one here gave orders to break into the damned Watergate. We're clean. It's only the Ellsberg thing, and if that comes out, it's 'national security'.

NIXON: 'Security' is not strong enough.

HALDEMAN: How 'bout a COMINT classification. We put it on the Huston plan. Even the designation is classified.

NIXON: 'National priority.'

EHRLICHMAN: 'Priority'? How about 'secret, top secret'?

DEAN: I was thinking 'sensitive.'

NIXON: 'National security priority restricted and controlled secret.'

HALDEMAN: We'll work on it. I say we cut ourselves loose from these clowns and that's all there is to it. *A beat. Nixon looks out at the Rose Garden.*

NIXON: It's more than that. It could be more than that. I want Hunt paid.

EHRLICHMAN: Uh, we've never done this before, sir . . . How do we pay? In . . . hundreds? *(smirks)* Do you fill a black bag full of unmarked bills?

NIXON *(snaps)*: This is not a joke, John!

EHRLICHMAN: No, sir.

NIXON: We should set up a Cuban defense fund on this; take care of all of them.

HALDEMAN: Should we talk to Trini about paying these guys? Or maybe Chotiner?

NIXON: No, keep Trini out of this. Chotiner's too old. And for God's sake, keep Colson out. *(including Dean)* It's time to baptize our young counsel. That means Dean can never talk about it. Attorney-client privilege. Get to it. And Dean – you stay close to this.

DEAN: Yes, sir, don't worry –
Prompted, Ehrlichman and Dean leave. When the door closes:

NIXON: Bob, did I approve the Ellsberg thing? You know, I'm glad we tape all these conversations because . . . I never approved that break-in at Ellsberg's psychiatrist. Or maybe I approved it after the fact? Someday we've got to start transcribing the tapes . . .

HALDEMAN: You approved that before the fact, because I went over it with you. But . . .

NIXON: Uh, no one, of course, is going to see these tapes, but . . .

HALDEMAN: That's right, and it's more a problem for Ehrlichman. He fixed Hunt up with the phony CIA ID's, but . . . what else does Hunt have on us?
Again, Nixon chooses not to answer.

NIXON: We've got to turn off the FBI. You just go to the CIA, Bob, and tell Helms that Howard Hunt is blackmailing the President. Tell him that Hunt and his Cuban friends know too damn much, and if he goes public, it would be a fiasco for the CIA. He'll know what I'm talking about.

HALDEMAN (*still confused*): All right.

NIXON: Play it tough. That's the way they play it and that's the way we're going to play it. Don't lie to Helms and say there's no involvement, but just say this is sort of a comedy of errors, bizarre, without getting into it. Say the President believes it's going to open up the whole Bay of Pigs thing again. Tell Helms he should call the FBI, call Pat Gray, and say that we wish for the sake of the country – don't go any further into this hanky-panky, period!

HALDEMAN: The Bay of Pigs? . . . That was Kennedy's screwup. How does that threaten us?

NIXON: Just do what I say, Bob.

HALDEMAN: Yes, sir, but . . . do you think Gray'll go for it?

NIXON: Pat Gray'll do anything we ask him. That's why I appointed him.

HALDEMAN: He'll need a pretext. He'll never figure one out for himself.

NIXON (*sighs*): Christ, you're right – Gray makes Jerry Ford look like Mozart. (*then*) Just have Helms call him. Helms can scare anybody.

HALDEMAN: The only problem with that, sir – it gets us into obstruction of justice.

NIXON: It's got nothing to do with justice. It's national security.

HALDEMAN: How is this national security?

NIXON: Because the President says it is. My job is to protect this country from its enemies, and its enemies are inside the walls.
Pause. Haldeman is perplexed.

NIXON: I suppose you thought the Presidency was above this sort of thing.

HALDEMAN: Sir?

NIXON: This isn't a 'moral' issue, Bob. We have to keep our enemies at bay or our whole program is gonna go down the tubes. The FBI is filled with people who're pissed that I put Gray in and not one of their own. Vietnam, China, the Soviet Union: when you look at the big picture, Bob, you'll see we're doing a hell of a lotta good in this world. Let's not screw it up with some shit-ass, third-rate burglary.

HALDEMAN: I'll talk to Helms. *(looks at his watch)* Oh, Pat asked if you're coming to the Residence for dinner tonight.

NIXON: No, no, not tonight. Don't let her in here; I have too much to do.

HALDEMAN: Yes, sir. I'll talk to Helms, and, uh . . .

what's our press position on this Watergate thing?
What do I tell Ziegler to tell them?

9. INT. THE WHITE HOUSE. LINCOLN SITTING ROOM.
NIGHT (1973).
RESUME SCENE – NIXON *takes another drink, looks
up at Lincoln's portrait.*

NIXON (*on the tape, yelling*): Tell 'em what we've always
    told 'em! Tell 'em anything but the Goddamn truth!
    *As the tape grinds on with hard-to-hear
    DIALOGUE, Nixon searches through a drawer in
    the rolltop desk next to the fireplace. He finds a
    small vial of pills, fumbles with the cap. He rips the
    cap off, the pills scattering on the desk.*

NIXON: Shit!
    *He begins scooping them back into the bottle, his
    hands trembling with the effort.*

NIXON (*mumbles*): Put me in this position . . . Expose
    me like this.
    He downs a couple of pills with the Scotch.

NIXON: Why don't they just fucking shoot me?
    Nixon takes another drink, looks down.
    SHARP CUTBACK TO:

10. INT. TV STUDIO. NIGHT (1960).
*DOCUMENTARY FOOTAGE – JOHN F. KENNEDY
looking straight at the camera. Tanned, impeccable,
confident.*

KENNEDY: I do not think the world can exist in the long run half-slave and half-free. The real issue before us is how we can prevent the balance of power from turning against us . . . If we sleep too long in the sixties, Mr. Khrushchev will 'bury' us yet . . . I think it's time America started moving again.

DISSOLVE TO:

NIXON *does not look well. His clothes are baggy, and he has a slight sheen of perspiration around his lower lip. He seems uncomfortable in his movements, robotic, falsely aggressive with his raised eyebrow and glaring demeanor. (The following essences are taken from four debates and various campaign material; in using a documentary 'JFK,' we will be cutting around him when off-debate material is used.)*

NIXON: . . .When it comes to experience, I want you to remember I've had 173 meetings with President Eisenhower, and 217 times with the National Security Council. I've attended 163 Cabinet meetings. I've visited fifty-four countries and had discussions with thirty-five presidents, nine prime ministers, two emperors, and the Shah of Iran . . .

11. INT. TV STUDIO. CONTROL ROOM. NIGHT.

PAT NIXON, *a year older than Dick, watches her champion through the glass booth. The 'Mona Lisa' of American politics, she projects deep admiration for, and pride in, her husband. But now she appears perturbed by what she's seeing.*

A younger HALDEMAN *sits watching the debates on monitors with* HERB KLEIN, *press secretary, and* OTHERS *in the Nixon circle. Through the glass we see the CANDIDATES.*

MURRAY CHOTINER, *campaign manager, overweight and bow-tied, moves down the row of monitors holding a cigar. He manages to drop ashes on an attractive KENNEDY STAFFER.*

CHOTINER: Excuse me, sweetheart.
As he sits next to Haldeman, Nixon drones on.

NIXON (*on TV monitor*): Let's take hydroelectric power. In our administration, we've built more . . .

CHOTINER (*privately*): Jesus Christ, has he told them how many pushups he can do yet? What the hell happened to him?

HALDEMAN: He just got out of the hospital, Murray, and he hasn't taken an hour off during the campaign, thanks to you.

CHOTINER: You could've at least gotten him a suit that fit, for Christ's sake, and slapped some makeup on him. He looks like a frigging corpse!

NIXON (*TV*): . . . When we consider the lineup of the world, we find there are 590 million people on our side, 800 million people on the Communist side, and 600 million who are neutral. The odds are 5 to 3 against us . . .

HALDEMAN: He wouldn't do the makeup. Said it was for queers.

JFK's face is on the monitors now.

CHOTINER: Kennedy doesn't look like a queer, does he? *(then)* He looks like a God.

HALDEMAN: Murray, it's not a beauty contest.

CHOTINER: We better hope not.

PAT *(upset)*: What are you doing to him, Murray?! Look at him – he's not well. He doesn't have to debate John Kennedy.

HALDEMAN: Mrs. Nixon, we didn't . . .

CHOTINER: Pat, baby, listen, when it comes to . . .

PAT: He can win without doing this.

KENNEDY *(TV)*: . . . in attacking my resolve, Mr. Nixon has carefully avoided mentioning my position on Cuba . . .

HALDEMAN: Oh shoot! He's going to do it! Here it comes.

KENNEDY *(TV)*: . . . As a result of administration policies, we have seen Cuba go to the Communists . . . eight jet minutes from the coast of Florida! Castro's influence will spread through all of Latin America. We must attempt to strengthen the democratic anti-Castro forces in exile. These fighters have had virtually no support from our government!

HALDEMAN (*whispers to Klein, Chotiner*): Sonofabitch! He was briefed last week by the CIA. He's using it against us! He knows we can't respond.

CHOTINER: It's a disgrace.

MODERATOR: Mr. Nixon?
Nixon looks, astounded, at JFK. He fumbles his response.

NIXON: I think . . . I think . . . that's the sort of very dangerous and irresponsible suggestion that . . . helping the Cuban exiles who oppose Castro would, uh . . . not only be a violation of international law, it would be . . .

HALDEMAN (*closes his eyes*): He's treading water. Don't mention Khrushchev.

NIXON: . . . an open invitation for Mr. Khrushchev to become involved in Latin America. We would lose all our friends in Latin America.

KLEIN: He just violated national security, Dick! Attack the bastard!

KENNEDY: I, for one, have never believed the foreign policy of the United States should be dictated by the Kremlin. As long as . . .
Klein hangs his head; Chotiner shares a look with Haldeman.
The young Kennedy staffers applaud gleefully.

NIXON (V.O.): The sonofabitch stole it!

12. INT. AMBASSADOR HOTEL. SUITE. LOS ANGELES. DAWN (1960).

NIXON *stands at the center of a room crowded with his MEN. He is despondent, astounded.* PAT NIXON *watches silently, bitter, nearly in tears.*

CHOTINER: He carried every cemetery in Chicago! And Texas – they had the Goddamned cattle voting!
The final ELECTION FIGURES are coming in over the television. They show Kennedy with a 120,000-voter margin – 34.2 to 34.1 million – and run down the electoral college votes.

CHOTINER: Closest election in history, Dick, and they stole it. Sonofabitch!

NIXON: He outspent us and he still cheated. A guy who's got everything. I can't believe it. We came to Congress together. I went to his wedding. We were like brothers, for Christ's sake.
Pat leaves abruptly; she can't take it anymore. Chotiner looks at Dick as if he were incredibly naive. HALDEMAN *and* KLEIN *are at a table, reams of returns before them.*

KLEIN: We've got the figures, Dick! The fraud is obvious – we call for a recount.

HALDEMAN: Nobody's ever contested a presidential election.

CHOTINER: Who's going to do the counting? The Democrats control Texas, they control Illinois.

KLEIN: We shift 25,000 votes in two states, and . . .

CHOTINER: How long would that take? Six months? A year?

HALDEMAN: Meanwhile, what happens to the country?

NIXON: That bastard! If I'd called his shot on Cuba I would've won. He made me look soft.

KLEIN (*reading transcript*): 'I feel sorry for Nixon because he does not know who he is, and at each stop he has to decide which Nixon he is at the moment, which must be very exhausting.' – Jack Kennedy.

CHOTINER: Bullshit!
The CAMERA is driving in on Nixon building to a rage. Klein knows how to get to him.

KLEIN (*reading*): 'Nixon's a shifty-eyed, Goddamn liar. If he had to stick to the truth he'd have very little to say. If you vote for him you ought to go to hell!' – Harry S. Truman . . . That's what killed us, Dick, not Cuba – the personality problem. Are we gonna let these sonofabitch Democrats get away with this?

HALDEMAN (*sotto voce*): You know, Herb, it's not the time . . . .
Nixon in close-up, inner demons moving him. A brief IMAGE of something ugly . . . in Nixon. Himself, perhaps, drenched in blood, or death imagery.

NIXON: Goddamn Kennedy! Goes to Harvard. His father

hands him everything on a silver platter! All my life they been sticking it to me. Not the right clothes, not the right schools, not the right family. And then he *steals* from me! I have *nothing* and *he steals*. *(softly, lethal)* . . . And he says I have 'no class.' And they love him for it. It's not fair, Murray, it's not fair.

CHOTINER: Dick, you're only forty-seven. You contest this election, you're finished. You gotta swallow this one. They stole it fair and square.
Nixon looks at him, broken-hearted. He controls his reaction, and exits the room.

CHOTINER: We'll get 'em next time, Dick.

KLEIN: What makes you think there's gonna be a next time, Murray?
Chotiner picks up the corner of a campaign poster with Nixon's face on it, the name in bold below.

CHOTINER: Because if he's not President Nixon, he's nobody.

13. INT. AMBASSADOR HOTEL. CORRIDOR & SUITE. DAWN.
NIXON *crosses the corridor which is subdued in the morning light. He hesitates at the door, knocks softly.*
    PAT NIXON *stirs quietly as her husband walks to her bed. They occupy separate beds.*

NIXON: We lost . . .

PAT *(bitterly)*: I know . . .

NIXON: It's hard to lose . . .

She reaches out to touch him. He allows himself to be touched. It seems that, between them, intimacy is difficult.

PAT: It makes us human . . .

NIXON: It's not fair, Buddy. I can take the insults; I can take the name-calling. But I can't take the losing. I hate it.

PAT: We don't *have* to put ourselves through this again, Dick.

NIXON: What do you mean? We worked for it. We earned it. It's ours.

PAT: It is. We know that. *(then)* And it's enough that we know. Just think of the girls. They're still young. We never see them. I lost my parents. I don't want them to lose theirs; I don't want them to grow up without a mother and father . . .

NIXON: Maybe I should get out of the game. What do you think, Buddy? Go back to being a lawyer and end up with something solid, some money at the end of the line . . . You know I keep thinking of my old man tonight. He was a failure too.

PAT: You're not a failure, Dick.

NIXON: You know how much money he had in the bank when he died? *(beat)* Nothing. He was so damned honest . . . *(then)* But I miss him. I miss him a hell of a lot.

He seems about to cry. Pat reaches out and cradles
his head on her shoulder. On his eyes we:
CUT TO:

14. EXT. NIXON GROCERY STORE. DUSK (1925).
A few gas pumps in front, overlooking a dry western,
Edward Hopper landscape. A run-down residence at the
back. A large man in a bloody butcher's apron, FRANK
NIXON *(46), crosses.*

15. INT. NIXON GROCERY STORE. DUSK.
HAROLD *(16), tall, handsome, walks in whistling. He*
winks at RICHARD *(12), who is sorting fruit in the bins.*
HANNAH *(39), a dour but gracious Quaker woman, is*
behind the counter with a CUSTOMER.

RICHARD *(whispers)*: What'd he say?

HAROLD: What do you think? He said in life there's no
free ride.

RICHARD: What'd you say?

HAROLD: I said I didn't need a ride. *(flashes a smile)* I
need a suit.
Richard buries his face in his hands.

RICHARD: Oh, no, Harold. He doesn't respond well to
humor. *(looks at his Mother, worried)* . . . Maybe if
you talk to Mother she can . . .

HAROLD: I'd rather get a whipping than have another

talk with her. *Anything* but a talk with her.
Richard is terrified Mom might overhear:

RICHARD: Shhhh!
*But it's too late. Hannah looks over, very sharp, as
her customer departs:*

HANNAH: Richard . . . come with me, would you . . .

RICHARD (*surprised, aloud*): Why me?

16. INT. NIXON HOUSE. KITCHEN. DUSK.
RICHARD, *obediently seated, pays his Mother heed. He
seems a gloomy, unsmiling child in her presence. We
sense that this is familiar territory for both.* HANNAH,
very quiet, penetrating with her gaze.

HANNAH: Because Harold tests thy father's will is no
    reason to admire him. Let Harold's worldliness be a
    warning to thee, not an example.

RICHARD: Yes, Mother . . .

HANNAH: Harold may have lost touch with his Bible,
    but thou must never lapse.
    Then, she extends her hand.

HANNAH: Now, give it to me . . .
    Richard is about to plead ignorance.

HANNAH: Do not tell a lie, Richard . . . The cornsilk
    cigarette Harold gave thee behind the store this
    morning.

RICHARD (*lying*): I don't . . . have them. Mother . . . I swear, I didn't smoke.

HANNAH (*withdrawing*): I see . . . Well then, Richard, we have nothing more to talk about, do we?

RICHARD (*fearful, blurts out*): Please, Mother, it . . . it was just one time, Mother, I'm . . . I'm sorry.

HANNAH: So am I. Thy father will have to know of thy lying.

RICHARD (*terrified*): No, no! Please, don't. Don't tell him. I'll never do it again. I promise. I promise . . . (*on the edge of tears*) Please, Mama . . .

HANNAH (*pause*): I expect more from thee, Richard. *He buries his head in her skirt. The faintest smile on Hannah's face as she pockets the cigarette.*

RICHARD: Please! I'll never let you down again, Mother. Never. I promise.

HANNAH: Then this shall be our little secret. (*She lifts his face to hers.*) Remember that I see into thy soul as God sees. Thou may fool the world. Even thy father. But not me, Richard. Never me.

RICHARD: Mother, think of me always as your faithful dog . . .

17. INT. NIXON HOUSE. KITCHEN. NIGHT.
HANNAH *puts the food on the table as* FRANK NIXON, *sleeves rolled up, waits at the head of the table, fuming.*

ARTHUR (6) *and* DONALD (9) *join* RICHARD *and*
HAROLD. *(The fifth brother, Edward, has not yet been
born.)*
   Hannah takes the remaining food to TWO HOBOS
*who are standing outside the kitchen door. Harold
reaches for his spoon impatiently.*

FRANK: Don't you dare, Harold!

HAROLD *(a little laugh)*: I just thought, since the food
   was here . . .

HANNAH: We haven't said grace yet. Richard.

RICHARD *(nervously)*: Is it my turn?
   *Hannah nods. Richard puts his hands together,
   trying to please.*

RICHARD: Heavenly Father, we humbly thank –

FRANK *(interrupts)*: I'll do it. There's a coupla things I
   wanna say.

HANNAH: Could thou at least remove thy apron, Frank?

FRANK: This blood pays the bills, Hannah. I'm not
   ashamed of how I earn my money. *(clears his throat)*
   Heavenly Father, you told Adam in the Garden, after
   that business with the snake, that man would have
   to earn his way by the sweat of his face. Well, as far
   as I can tell, Father, what was true in Eden is true in
   Whittier, California. So we ask you now to remind
   certain of our young people . . . *(glares at Harold)*
   That the *only* way to get a new suit to go to the
   promenade with Margaret O'Herlihy, who happens

41

to be a Catholic by the way, is to *work for it. (then)* Amen.
Little cute-faced Arthur looks up.

ARTHUR: I like Margaret O'Herlihy too. She's very pretty. Can we pray now?
The boys start giggling.

HANNAH: Arthur!

FRANK: You think this is funny? *(then)* Pretty soon you boys are gonna have to get out there and scratch, 'cause you're not gonna get anywhere on your good looks. Just ask those fellas . . .
Frank waves to the Hobos, now squatting and wolfing down the food. They look up, embarrassed.

FRANK: Charity is only gonna get you so far – even with saints like your mother around. Struggle's what gives life meaning, not victory – struggle. When you quit struggling, they've beaten you, and then you end up in the street with your hand out.
Frank begins eating; the rest follow.

NIXON *(V.O.)*: My mother was a saint, but my old man struggled his whole life. You could call him a little man, a poor man, but they never beat him. I always tried to remember that when things didn't go my way . . .

18. EXT. WHITTIER FOOTBALL FIELD. DAY (1932).
FOOTBALL MONTAGE: RICHARD *(19)*, 150 *pounds, is*

on the defensive line as the ball is hiked. ('Let's get fired
up!') He gets creamed by a 200-pound offensive tackle.
He jumps up, no face guard, hurting, and resets. AD LIB
football chatter. We can tell from Richard's cheap
uniform that he is a substitute. But:

We go again. And again. Building a special
RHYTHM of JUMP CUTS showing Nixon getting
mauled each time. He doesn't have a chance, this kid,
but he has pluck. And he comes back for more. And
more.

This image of pain and humiliation should weave
itself in and out of the film in repetitive currents. As we
CUT TO:

19. OMIT #19

20. INT. HILTON HOTEL. BALLROOM. NIGHT (1962).
We move down past a blizzard of balloons and confetti
blown by a hotel air-conditioner to a huge 'NIXON
FOR GOVERNOR' banner.

NIXON thrusts his arms in the air – the twin-V salute.
The CROWD cheers wildly. SUBTITLE READS:
'CALIFORNIA GOVERNORSHIP, 1962.'

21. INT. HILTON HOTEL. SUITE. NIGHT.
NIXON is slumped in an armchair, feet on a coffee table,
holding a drink, going through defeat once again.

HALDEMAN stares glumly at the TV. PAT sits across
the room in grim silence.

ON TV – *a* NEWSCASTER *stands in front of a tally board with the network logo: 'Decision '62.'*

NEWSCASTER: President Kennedy has called Governor Pat Brown to congratulate him . . .

HALDEMAN: Are we making a statement?

NEWSCASTER: ABC is now projecting that Brown will defeat Richard Nixon by more than a quarter of a million votes.
NIXON *holds up his drink to the screen. Moves to a piano.*

NIXON: Thank you, Fidel Castro.

PAT: You're not going to blame this on Castro, are you?

NIXON: I sure am. The Goddamned missile crisis united the whole country behind Kennedy. And he was supporting Brown. People were scared, that's why.

PAT: I suppose Castro staged the whole thing just to beat you.

NIXON: Buddy, before you join the jubilation at my being beaten again, you should remember: People vote not out of love, but *fear*. They don't teach that at Sunday School or at the Whittier Community Playhouse!

HALDEMAN (*interjects*): I should go down and check in with our people.
Haldeman leaves quickly.
ON TV: GOVERNOR BROWN *steps to the*

podium. A band plays 'Happy Days Are Here Again.'

PAT (*back at Dick*): I'm glad they don't. You forget I had a life before California, a rough, rough life. Life isn't always fair, Dick . . .
Nixon drowns her out, playing the piano (well) and singing along bitterly.

NIXON: ' – the skies above are clear again. Let's sing a song of cheer again – ' . . . Cocksucker!
Pat turns off the TV.

NIXON (*continues to play*): Don't you want to listen to Brown's victory speech?

PAT: No. I'm not going to listen to any more speeches ever again.

NIXON: Amen to that.

PAT: It's over, Dick.

NIXON: I'll concede in the morning.

PAT: Not that. (*then*) Us.
Nixon stops playing, looks at her.

PAT (*coldly*): I've always stood by you. I campaigned for you when I was pregnant. During Checkers, when Ike wanted you out, I told you to fight. This is different, Dick. You've changed. You've grown more bitter, like you're at war with the world. You weren't that way before. You scare me sometimes . . . I'm fifty years old now, Dick. How many people's hands have I shaken – people I didn't like, people I didn't even know. It's as if, I don't know, I went to sleep a long time ago and missed the years between . . . I've had enough.

He moves towards her awkwardly. Pat struggles. She goes to a window, her back to him. She is not one to enjoy 'scenes.' She tends to accommodate to others to preserve an aura of happiness.

NIXON (*confused*): What are you saying? What are you talking about?

PAT: I want a divorce.

NIXON: My God – divorce? *(beat)* . . . What about the girls?

PAT: The girls will grow up. They only know you from television anyway.

NIXON: It would ruin us, Buddy, our family.

PAT: You're ruining us. If we stay with you, you'll take us down with you. *(beat)* This isn't political, Dick. This is our life.

NIXON: Everything's political, for Christ's sake! I'm political. And you're political too!

PAT: No, I'm not! I'm finished.
She is very serious. He sees it. It terrifies him. The same withdrawal he experienced from his mother.

NIXON: This is just what they want, Buddy. Don't you see? They want to drive us apart. To beat us. We can't let them do it. We've been through too much together, Buddy . . . We belong together.

PAT (*ironic*): That's what you said the first time we met. You didn't even know me.
MARRIAGE MONTAGE: During this scene we have a series of SHOTS of their courtship – the Whittier College campus, 1930s Los Angeles; driving in a car together; the wedding; the FIRST CHILD; the Pacific NAVAL CAPTAIN underneath a palm tree; running as a first-time CONGRESSMAN with Pat; the EISENHOWER years . . .

NIXON (*very tender*): Oh, yes I did. I told you I was gonna marry you, didn't I? On the first date . . . I said it because I knew . . . I knew you were the one . . . so solid and so strong . . . and so beautiful. You were the most beautiful thing I'd ever seen . . . I don't want to lose you, Buddy, ever . . .
INTERCUT WITH:
NIXON *seeking tenderness. He puts a hand on her arm. He tries gently to pull her towards him, to kiss her.*

PAT: Dick, don't . . .

NIXON: Buddy, look at me . . . just look at me. Do you really want me to quit?
She stares out the window. A long moment.

PAT: We can be happy. We really can. We love you, Dick. The girls and I . . .

NIXON: If I stop . . . there'll be no more talk of divorce?

A long moment. She finally turns her eyes to him, assenting.

NIXON: I'll do it. *(waves his hand)* No more.

PAT: Are you serious?

NIXON: Yeah . . . I'm out.

PAT: Is that the truth?

NIXON: I'll never run again. I promise.
   SHARP CUT TO:

22. INT. HILTON HOTEL. HALLWAY. NIGHT.
NIXON *stalks down the hallway, fuming.* HALDEMAN *walks alongside.*

NIXON: Where are they?

HALDEMAN *(worried, points to a door)*: Dick, you don't
   have to make a statement. Herb covered it for you.

NIXON: No!
   He bursts through the door into:

23. INT. HILTON HOTEL. PRESS CONFERENCE. BALLROOM.
NIGHT.
A noisy CROWD of REPORTERS reacts, excitedly, to
NIXON's *fast entry. The smell of blood in the air.*
   TIME CUT TO:
   NIXON *at the podium.*

NIXON: . . . I believe Governor Brown has a heart, even though he believes I do not. I believe he is a good American, even though he feels I am not. I am proud of the fact that I defended my opponent's patriotism; you gentlemen didn't report it but I am proud I did that. And I would appreciate it, for once, gentlemen, if you would write what I say. (*time dissolve*) . . . For sixteen years, ever since the Hiss case, you've had a lot of fun – a lot of fun. But recognize you have a responsibility, if you're against a candidate, to give him the shaft, but if you do that, at least put one lonely reporter on the campaign who will report what the candidate says now and then . . .

HALDEMAN *glances at* KLEIN.

NIXON: . . . I think all-in-all I've given as good as I've taken. But as I leave you I want you to know – just think how much you're going to be missing: you won't have Nixon to kick around anymore. Because, gentlemen, this is my last press conference . . .

A FEW REPORTERS shout questions. There is a loud confusion, but Nixon has vanished.

KLEIN: What the hell was that?

HALDEMAN (*beat*): Suicide.

CUT TO:
NIXON HISTORICAL MONTAGE:
A grainy 'NEWSREEL' treats NIXON as political history, now over. The ANONYMOUS REPORTERS return – YOUNG NIXON, in his

49

*Navy uniform, is campaigning in California in the
1940s against Voorhis and Douglas.*

REPORTER 1 (V.O.): We can now officially write the
political obituary of Richard Milhous Nixon . . . He
came into being as part of the big post-war 1946
Republican sweep of the elections. People were
weary of the New Deal and FDR's big government . . .
*Images of FDR, TRUMAN, and ACHESON, early
Cold War imagery – the Soviets, Berlin.*

REPORTER 1 (V.O.): . . . The United States had been a
strong ally of the Soviet Union, which had lost more
than twenty million people in its fight against
Nazism. But Nixon, coming from the South Pacific
war, won his first term in the House by freely
associating his liberal opponent, Jerry Voorhis, with
Communism.
*Images of Voorhis, Hoover . . . NIXON working a
CROWD, standing on the tailgate of a station-
wagon, debating Voorhis.*

REPORTER 2 (V.O.): For Nixon, politics was war. He
didn't have opponents, he had enemies. He didn't
run against people, he ruined them . . . He won his
California seat in the U.S. Senate in 1950 in a vicious
campaign against liberal congresswoman and movie
actress, Helen Gahagan Douglas . . .
*NEWSFILM of NIXON and CHOTINER at a rally
with PAT. Images of DOUGLAS follow.
CAMPAIGN WORKERS handing out smear
literature.*

NIXON ('*newsfilm look*'): How can Helen Douglas, capable actress that she is, take up so strange a role as a foe of Communism? Why, she's pink right down to her underwear . . .

REPORTER 3 (*V.O.*): . . . Nixon quickly became the Republicans' attack dog. He tore into Truman for losing Mainland China in 1949, and blamed the war in Korea on a weak foreign policy. His speeches, if more subtle than those of his Republican ally, Joe McCarthy, were just as aggressive . . .
Nixon at another rally with Pat.

NIXON ('*newsfilm look*'): . . . I promise to continue to expose the people that have sold this country down the river! Until we have driven all the crooks and Communists and those that have helped them out of office!!
Images of Truman, the hydrogen bomb, the Rosenbergs, Klaus Fuchs, Oppenheimer, the Chinese taking over in 1949 . . . Mao.

NIXON ('*newsfilm look*'): The direct result of Truman's decisions is that China has gone Communist. Mao is a monster. Why?! Why, Mr. Acheson?! Who in the State Department is watching over American interests?! Who has given the Russians the atomic bomb?! . . . Today the issue is slavery! The Soviet Union is an example of the slave state in its ultimate development. Great Britain is halfway down the same road; powerful interests are striving to impose the British socialist system upon the people of the United States!

REPORTER 2 (*V.O.*): . . . Nixon became one of the leading lights on the notorious House Un-American Activities Committee, questioning labor leaders, Spanish Civil War veterans, Hollywood celebrities . . .

NIXON (*questioning witness*): Can you tell me today the names of any pictures which Hollywood has made in the last five years showing the evils of totalitarian Communism?
Nixon surrounded by Reporters outside the HUAC hearing room.

REPORTER 4 (*V.O.*): . . . but it was the Alger Hiss case that made Nixon a household name . . .
IMAGES of Alger Hiss's career: clerking for Oliver Wendell Holmes; with FDR at Yalta, with Churchill, with Stalin.

REPORTER 4 (*V.O.*): . . . One of the architects of the United Nations, intimate of FDR and Oliver Wendell Holmes, Alger Hiss was a darling of the liberals. (*then*) But Whittaker Chambers, a former freelance journalist, said he was a Communist.
WHITTAKER CHAMBERS testifying before HUAC.

CHAMBERS (*TV interview*): . . . if the American people understood the real character of Alger Hiss, they would boil him in oil . . .

REPORTER 4 (*V.O.*): . . . Hiss claimed he was being set

up by Nixon and J. Edgar Hoover to discredit the New Deal's policies. The case came down to an Underwood typewriter, and a roll of film hidden in a pumpkin patch.

DOCUMENTARY IMAGE – A DETECTIVE-TYPE reaches into a hollowed-out pumpkin and pulls out microfilm . . . In his congressional office, Nixon examines the film with a magnifying glass, playing to the cameras with a deadly serious mien . . . Shots of MRS. HISS, the Underwood typewriter.

REPORTER 4 (V.O.): . . . Years later the Freedom of Information Act revealed that the film showed a report on business conditions in Manchuria, and fire extinguishers on a U.S. destroyer. None of these documents was classified. Were they planted by Chambers, who seemed to have a strange, almost psychotic fixation with Alger Hiss?

NIXON (*'newsfilm'*): I asked Hiss if he'd ever known Chambers before. When he said 'no,' that's when I knew he was lying. That's when I knew I had him . . . He was twisting, turning, evading, changing his story to fit the evidence he knew we had . . . But I tell you this: I vow that we're going to go after everyone responsible for selling this country down the river. . . *NIXON points to a headline – 'Hiss Convicted'*

REPORTER 1 (V.O.): After two confusing trials, Hiss went to jail for perjury. To the right wing, Nixon was a hero and a patriot. To the liberals, he was a shameless self-promoter who had vengefully

destroyed a fine man. Eleanor Roosevelt angrily condemned him. It was to become a pattern: you either loved Richard Nixon or you hated him.
A brief IMAGE here that will recur throughout the film. An image of evil – call it 'The Beast.'

REPORTER 2 (*V.O.*): Driven by demons that seemed more personal than political, his rise was meteoric. Congressman at 33, senator at 35, Eisenhower's vice-presidential candidate at 39. Then came the Checkers Crisis . . . Nixon was accused of hiding a secret slush fund. About to be kicked off the ticket by Ike, he went on national television in an unprecedented appearance . . .
INTERCUT Checkers speech – Nixon, looking and sounding like Uriah Heep, pleads with the American people on TV, as Pat sits uncomfortably in an armchair nearby.

NIXON (*on TV*): . . . so now what I am going to do is to give this audience a complete financial history. Everything I've earned, everything I've spent, everything I owe . . .
Nixon forces a smile. Pat is clearly in pain, mortified.

REPORTER 2 (*V.O.*): The list included their house, their Oldsmobile, Pat's Republican cloth coat, and lastly, in what was to become history – a sentimental gift from a Texas businessman . . .

NIXON (*on TV*): You know what it was? It was a little cocker spaniel dog. Black and white spotted. And . . . our little girl, Tricia, the six-year-old, named it

'Checkers.' And you know, the kids love that dog and we're going to keep it . . .

REPORTER 4 (V.O.): Fifty-eight million people saw it. It was shameless. It was manipulative. *(then)* It was a huge success!
DOCUMENTARY REPLACEMENT – Nixon with Ike in triumph. A clip of Eisenhower praising Nixon. Nixon and Pat standing up to rock-throwing STUDENTS in Venezuela. Pointing his finger at KHRUSHCHEV in the Kitchen Debate.

REPORTER 3 (V.O.): Eisenhower put Nixon back on the ticket . . . Responding to attacks on Truman, Acheson, and the entire Democratic Party for betraying American principles in China, Korea, and elsewhere it was two-time Democratic presidential candidate, Adlai Stevenson, who perhaps best summed up the national unease with Richard Nixon . . .
DOCUMENTARY-SHOTS of ADLAI STEVENSON campaigning in '52 and '56 against IKE. Images of JOE McCARTHY precede. The HERBLOCK CARTOON of Nixon crawling out of the sewer system. Others of his cartoons follow.

STEVENSON (*radio V.O.*): . . . This is a man of many masks. Who can say they have seen his real face? He is on an ill-will tour, representing McCarthyism in a white collar. Nixonland has no standard of truth but convenience, and no standard of morality except the sly innuendo, the poison pen, the anonymous phone

call; the land of smash and grab and anything to win
. . . 'What, ultimately, shall it profit a man if he shall
gain the whole world and lose his own soul?'
*Ending with more recent SHOTS of Nixon
campaigning in '60 and '62. As the IMAGES spot out
in newsreel style:*

REPORTER 4 (V.O.): It was a great story of its time and,
in California where it started, it has come to a
crashing end. It is too bad in a way, because the
truth is, we never knew who Richard Nixon really
was. And now that he is gone, we never will . . .
*'March of Time'-type music as we SLOWLY FADE
INTO:*

NIXON (V.O.): 'Your father stinks' . . . They actually
said this to Tricia. Two girls wearing Kennedy pins.
At Chapin!

24. INT. FIFTH AVE APARTMENT. NEW YORK CITY. NIGHT
(1963).
*A New York cocktail party. Society DAMES. Rich,
conservative BUSINESSMEN, platters of martinis and
hors d'oeuvres carried by white-gloved BLACK
BUTLERS. The fashions are Balenciaga and Courreges,
tipping to the shorter hemlines; the mood is smoky and
upbeat, the folks pressed into airtight packs of loud
conversation.*

NIXON *is talking to* JOHN MITCHELL (54), *his wife*
MARTHA (40's), *and TWO OTHER ASSOCIATES of the
law firm he has joined.*

NIXON (*anguished*): She was crying when she came home (*shakes his head*). She was devastated.

MARTHA: Poor little Tricia! Well, that's New York – makes for a tougher animal later in life.

NIXON (*to the other lawyers*): I told her, her daddy couldn't even get a Goddamned job in this city when I got out of Duke. Every white-shoe lawyer firm turned me down. Didn't have the right 'look.' Hell, I couldn't even get into the FBI.

MITCHELL (*indicating*): Dick, we should catch Rocky 'fore he leaves.
NELSON ROCKEFELLER, *Governor of New York, dominates the room. Big smile, horn-rimmed glasses. Next to him is* HAPPY, *his new wife, much younger.*

NIXON (*glancing*): Well, he can walk in this direction too.

MARTHA: Did you catch that picture of you in the *News* last week, Dick? You were standing in a crowd on Fifth Avenue, and you were looking straight ahead, and everyone else was looking the other way like you'd just farted or something. (*laughs*) It said: 'Who Remembers Dick Nixon?' I was screaming. It was so funny!

NIXON: Yeah, that was hilarious, Martha. (*for the others*) They were all looking the other way 'cause they were waiting for the light to change. I called AP on that – typical of the press in this country, they wouldn't correct it. That or they print the retraction right next to the girdle ads.

LAWYER: Oh, I've read some very nice things about you.

MARTHA (*puts her hand on Nixon's arm*): Maybe where you come from. But where I come from, Dick Nixon is as misunderstood as a fox in a henhouse. And you know why? (*they all wait*) Because, honey, they all think your smile and your face are never in the same place at the same time. (*nervous laughter*) You and me – we gotta work on that, sweetie . . .

MITCHELL (*guiding Dick away*): Someone freshen Martha's drink. I think she's down a quart.

MARTHA: Well, zippety-fucking-doo-dah!
Mitchell moves Nixon away towards the Rockefeller GROUP.

MITCHELL: Sorry, Dick. She's a little tipsy.

NIXON: You mean *smashed!* She called up at *midnight* last week. Talking a bunch of crap! Pat can't stand her.

MITCHELL: It's a thing she does. She talks at night.

NIXON: Talks all day too! How the hell can you put up with her, John?

MITCHELL (*sheepishly*): What the hell – I love her. And she's great in bed.
Rockefeller holds court, not immediately noticing Nixon.

ROCKEFELLER: . . . There are no guarantees in politics.
I'm going to roll the dice with everyone else.
HENRY KISSINGER *(40's), intense, holds a martini.*

KISSINGER: Well, if a Rockefeller can't become President
of the United States, what's the point of democracy?
(laughter)

NIXON: The point of democracy is that even the son of a
grocer can become president. *(laughs)*

ROCKEFELLER: And you came damn close, too, Dick.
*As Rocky clutches Dick, who doesn't like to be
touched:*

ROCKEFELLER: Howya doin'! New York treating you
okay? I'm sorry I haven't been able to see you at
all . . .

NIXON *(cutting off the apology)*: Well enough. You're
looking 'happy,' Nelson. *(with a look to Happy)*

ROCKEFELLER: Oh, Happy! *(introduces his new wife)*
Dick Nixon . . .You remember him.

NIXON: Hi, Happy. Well, you're obviously making him
happy.

ROCKEFELLER: Repartee, Dick – very good. Hey, I feel
ten years younger! It makes a helluva, difference, let
me tell ya! How's the lawyer life?

NIXON: Never made so much money in my life. But my
upbringing doesn't allow me to enjoy it. I did get to
argue a case before the Supreme Court.

ROCKEFELLER: Won or lost?

NIXON: Lost.

ROCKEFELLER: Someday, Dick.
OTHERS are pressing in on Rockefeller, who is obviously the 'star' of the party, so there is pressure to talk fast.

NIXON: But being out of the game gives me time to write.

ROCKEFELLER: To what?

NIXON: Write. You know, a book. I'm calling it 'Six Crises.' It's a good thing, Rocky – take some time off to write.

ROCKEFELLER (*shaking another hand*): Hiya, fellow . . . What were they?

NIXON: What?

ROCKEFELLER: The 'crises'?

NIXON: 'Checkers' of course, Hiss, Ike's heart attack, Venezuela, the Kitchen Debate, and Kennedy.

ROCKEFELLER: Sounds like you got a crisis syndrome. Aren't you exaggerating a bit, Dick? Call it three-and-a-half, maybe four . . .

NIXON (*laughs awkwardly*): Let's wait and see how you survive *your* first crisis, Rocky . . .

ROCKEFELLER: Whatcha mean by that?

NIXON: You know: how the voters are gonna play your divorce.
Rockefeller, who still clutches the visibly uncomfortable Nixon, gives him a squeeze before finally releasing him.

ROCKEFELLER: Don't you worry about it, fellah, and I won't. *(about to rejoin his wife)*

NIXON *(smiling)*: Well, in any case, Rocky, I'll send you my book. 'Six Crises.'

ROCKEFELLER *(pauses, aside)*: Whatcha predicting – your boy Goldwater's going to split the party?

NIXON: Some say *you* are, Rocky.

ROCKEFELLER: The Republican Party was never a home to extremists. You should know better. This guy's as stupid as McCarthy, and McCarthy never did you any good in the long run, now did he?
A pause. It lands home on Dick. Rockefeller turns to Kissinger, who's been listening.

ROCKEFELLER: Hey, you know Henry Kissinger – he's down from Harvard. On my staff, foreign policy whiz . . .

NIXON *(shakes hands)*: No, but I liked your book on nuclear weapons. We have similar views on the balance of power . . .

ROCKEFELLER: Well, that's wonderful. So get me this 'crisis' thing, Dick; I'll be glad to take a look at it.

He raps Nixon one more time on the shoulder and moves off into a waiting GROUP.

NIXON: . . . as the old alliances crumble.

KISSINGER: Finally someone who's noticed! I'm a great admirer of yours too, Mr. Nixon. You are an unusual politician. We share a mutual idol – 'Six Crises' sounds like a page from Churchill.

NIXON: Churchill, De Gaulle, Disraeli. They all went through the pain of losing power.

KISSINGER (*smiles*): But they all got it back again, didn't they? (*proffering a card*) We should have lunch sometime.
TIME CUT:
NIXON *and* MITCHELL *move to the edges of the* PARTY, *which is now diminishing. They bypass* PAT, *who is absently staring off in conversation with* MARTHA *and SEVERAL OTHER LADIES who lunch . . . Nixon looks back at* ROCKEFELLER *leaving* – KISSINGER *hovering near him.*

NIXON (*seething*): Rocky's full of shit! No way he's going to get nominated west of the Hudson with a new wife. He's gonna be drinking Scotches in retirement at some Goddamn country club with the rest of the Republicans.

MITCHELL: Goes to show you all the moolah in the world can't buy you a brain.

NIXON (*snags a drink from a passing tray*): Well, he
   seems to have bought Kissinger.

MITCHELL: The Jewboy's a Harvard whore with the
   morals of an eel – sells himself to the highest bidder.

NIXON (*brays loudly*): You're the one who should be in
   politics, John. You're tougher than I am. You never
   crack.

MITCHELL: That'll be the day.

NIXON: Let's get out of here; it's too painful. I hate it.
   (*then*) We went bowling last weekend. Next
   weekend we're going to the zoo. Whoever said there
   was life after politics was full of shit.

MITCHELL: Make some money, Dick, prove yourself to
   the Wall Street crowd and let Goldwater and
   Rockefeller take the fall against Kennedy.
   Nixon looks at him.

NIXON: Yeah. John, I'm in hell. (*then*) I'll be mentally
   dead in two years and physically dead in four. I miss
   – I don't know – making love to the people. I miss –
   entering a room. I miss – the pure 'acting' of it.
   John, I've got to get back in the arena.
   On Pat glancing over:
   CUT TO:

25. INT. DALLAS CONVENTION SITE. DAY (1963).
*SPOTLIGHT on a sexy Studebaker car of the era. A
DRUM ROLL, and suddenly out of the various*

apertures of the car pop six half-naked HOSTESSES doing the twist. Wild cheers.

The ANNOUNCER describes the new gimmicks on the car (AD LIB) as we swing to reveal NIXON, *looking uncomfortable in a Stetson cowboy hat shaking hands with AUTOGRAPH SEEKERS and car buffs, posing for cheesecake photographs. A banner behind him reveals: 'Dallas Welcomes Studebaker Dealers.'*

The Studebaker GIRLS are fanning out through the sales booths, whistling, swinging whips, as a large man in a Stetson, JACK JONES, *accompanied by a suave-looking Cuban-born businessman,* TRINI CARDOZA, *breaks through the autograph hounds to rescue Nixon.*

JONES: That's enough now, let him be. He's just like you and me, folks, just another lawyer . . . Let's go, let's go, break it up . . .
    Moving Nixon out of there.

NIXON: Thanks, Jack. You sure throw a helluva party.

JONES: Party ain't started yet, Dick. Got these gals coming over to the ranch later for a little private 'thing,' y'know . . . There's some fellows I want you to meet.

NIXON: Well, uh, Trini and I have an early plane. We were hoping to get back to New York in time for . . .

TRINI: It'll be okay, Dick; these guys are interesting . . . real quiet. And the girls are too.

JONES: Y'know, it's not every day we Texans get to entertain the future President of the United States.

NIXON: Like you said Jack, I'm just a New York lawyer now.

JONES (*chuckles, with a look to Trini*): We'll see about that.
New FANS circle up, their WIVES giggling.

FANS: Oh, Mr. Nixon, could you sign . . .? My wife and I think you are just the greatest. Please run again . . .
More fans flood in, encircling him. On Trini and Jack watching this.

26. EXT. JONES RANCH. DAY.
An entire LONGHORN STEER turns on a spit in a large barbecue pit, basted by black SERVANTS. We see a sprawling Spanish-style RANCH HOUSE in the countryside. The parking area looks like a Cadillac dealership. The CROWD is a mixture of CORPORATE EXECUTIVES, CUBANS, and COWBOY-TYPES, some WIVES.

TRINI is talking to TWO of the DANCERS, nodding his head in NIXON's direction. They look, and smile at him.

Across the lawn, Nixon smiles back awkwardly as JACK JONES nudges him. They both eat steaks and corncobs.

JONES: I know for a fact the one with the big tits is a Republican, and she'd do anything for the Party.

NIXON: She's quite pretty.

JONES: Her name's Sandy . . .
    Trini joins them, bringing the girls.

NIXON: By the way, Jack, this looks like a pretty
    straightforward transaction to me, but we should get
    into it soon – take just a few minutes, maybe up at
    the house . . .

JONES (*to Trini, coming up*): He's all business, ain't he,
    Trini? (*to Dick*) Dick, we could've had our own
    Goddamn lawyers handle this deal. We brought you
    down here 'cause we wanted to talk to you . . .

TRINI: Dick, this is Teresa, and this is Sandy.

TERESA: Hi . . . Dick.

SANDY: Hi.

NIXON: Hello . . .
    Pause.

27. INT. JONES RANCH. DAY
*A walk-in stone fireplace dominates the room; the heavy
beams hung with black wrought-iron candelabras. Thick
cigar smoke impregnates the air, the crowd has
substantially thinned to the heaviest hitters. The MEN,
now in shirtsleeves, drink from bottles of bourbon . . .*
    *A man – MITCH – emerges from one of the side rooms
with a DANCER.*
    *Off to the side in a semi-private alcove, SANDY, the
dancer, tries to make conversation, but NIXON is
showing her a picture of his kids.*

66

NIXON: That's Julie . . . and that's Tricia. She, uh, reminds me a little bit of you . . .

SANDY (*'interested'*): Oh yeah . . . she really is . . . wholesome.
Trini interjects, trying to help out.

TRINI: So what's up? . . . Uh, I get the feeling Sandy really likes you, Dick.

SANDY: I like that name, Dick.

TRINI: Why don't you two disappear in the bedroom there. Come back in half an hour . . .

NIXON: Uh . . . Trini.
Trini smiles and, leaving Dick the playing field, vanishes. Sandy, feeling the vacuum, holds Nixon's hand.

SANDY: What do you say? Do you like me, Mister *Vice* President?
Nixon swallows hard, blushing now. He sweats, very uncomfortable with this intimacy.
NIXON (*croaks*): Yes, of course. But . . . uh . . .
A brief IMAGE flashes by – beastlike, offensive, unworthy.

NIXON: . . . I don't really know you yet, Sandy . . . What do you like? I mean, what kind of clothes do you like? Do you like blue . . . red?

SANDY: Oh, I like satin, I like pink . . .

NIXON: What kind of, uh . . . music do you like?

SANDY: I like jazz . . .

NIXON: Yeah . . . Guy Lombardo . . .

SANDY: Elvis I like too.

NIXON: Oh yeah, he's good.
Sandy puts her hand on his face and head.

SANDY: . . . but it depends what I'm doing to the music,
Dick . . .

NIXON: Uh, is your mother . . . still alive?

SANDY: Yeah, she lives in Dallas . . .

NIXON: She must be very attractive. Would she like an
autograph? She might remember me . . . Where's
Trini? *(looking around desperately)*
TIME CUT TO:

28.
*Later. The crowd has thinned further to a hard-core
dozen. The last man – Mitch – comes from the inner
bedrooms, zipping up; the Servants, chasing out the
straggling Girls. Another round of drinks is served. The
cigars are out.*

JONES: Hell, Kennedy's pissed Cuba away to the
Russians. And he don't know what the hell he's
doing in Vietnam. These are dangerous times, Dick,
especially for business . . .

NIXON: Agreed.

A CUBAN *in an Italian suit, one part sleazy, another part dangerous, steps from the shadows.*

CUBAN: We know what you tried to do for Cuba, Mr. Nixon. If you'd been elected in '60, we know Castro'd be dead by now.
NIXON *shares a look with* TRINI.

NIXON: Gentlemen, I tried. I told Kennedy to go into Cuba. He heard me and he made his decision. I appreciate your sentiments, I've heard them from many fine Cuban patriots, but it's nothing I can do anything about. Now, it's a long drive back to Dallas tonight, and Trini and I have got an early flight tomorrow to New York . . .

JONES (*interrupting*): Dick, these boys want you to run. (*The 'boys' mutter in unison.*) They're serious. They can deliver the South and they can put Texas in your column. That would've done it in '60.

NIXON: Only if Kennedy dumps Johnson.

JONES: That sonofabitch Kennedy is coming back down here tomorrow. Dick, we're willing to put up a shitpot fulla money to get rid of him – more money'n you ever dreamed of.

NIXON: Nobody's gonna beat Kennedy in '64 with all the money in the world.
A beat.

CUBAN: Suppose Kennedy don't run in '64?

*Nixon looks at him. A subconscious IMAGE again –
something slimy, reptilian.*

NIXON: Not a chance.

CUBAN: These are dangerous times, Mr. Nixon.
Anything can happen.
*Another pause. Nixon gathers together his papers
and briefcase.*

NIXON: Yes, well . . . Gentlemen, I promised my wife.
I'm out of politics.

MITCH (*insolent smile*): You just came down here for the
weather, right, Mr. Nixon?

NIXON: I came down here to close a deal for Studebaker.

TRINI: What about '68, Dick?

NIXON: Five years, Trini? In politics, that's an eternity.

JONES: Your country needs you, Dick.
Nixon shakes his hand, departs.

NIXON: Unfortunately, the country isn't available right
now.

29. EXT. LOVE FIELD. DAY (1963).
*A CROWD is waiting for Air Force One. People hold
banners, signs: 'Dallas Loves JFK,' 'We Love You
Jackie.'*
    A Cadillac pulls up at the far corner of the tarmac.

NIXON *gets out with* CARDOZA. *They walk toward a small executive* PLANE.

   Nixon pauses, looks up. He feels something ominous in the air.

NIXON: Trini, let's get out of here fast. Go check on the
   pilot, or they'll hold us up till he's out of the airport.
   *As Trini hurries off to the plane, Nixon takes one
   last look up at his fate written in the soft white
   clouds over Dallas. As we:*
   CUT TO:

30.
DOCUMENTARY – JOHN KENNEDY *coming off the
plane at Love Field with* JACKIE, *waving to the crowd.
The sound of a rushing, monstrous engine. Then wind.*

CUT TO:

31. INT. NIXON'S FIFTH AVENUE APARTMENT. DAY (1963).
NIXON *sits, subdued, in an armchair in a small study,
caught between the fire in the grate, the* TELEVISION
images of the assassination, and the phone call he's on.

NIXON (*low-key*): Look, Edgar, these guys were really
   strange, I mean, y'know . . . extremists, right-wing
   stuff, Birchers . . . Yeah? (*listens several beats*)
   PAT, *smoking nervously, watches from another
   chair. Newspapers are strewn all around.*
   DOCUMENTARY IMAGES *on the TV show a*

grieving JACKIE, BOBBY, TEDDY, and the TWO CHILDREN.

NIXON: I see . . . Oswald's got a Cuba connection to Castro? I see. A real Communist. That makes sense. Thank you, Edgar.
He hangs up. It's evident he's still puzzled, but wants to believe.

NIXON: Hoover says this Oswald checks out as a beatnik-type, a real bum, pro-Castro . . .
TV images of BOBBY KENNEDY.

PAT: Dick, you should call Bobby.

NIXON: He doesn't want me at the funeral.

PAT: You don't have to go.

NIXON (*glances at TV*): De Gaulle's gonna be there. And Macmillan. And Adenauer. Nixon can't *not* be there.

PAT: Then call him. I'm sure it was an oversight.

NIXON: No. It's his way. He hates me. Him and Teddy. They always hated me.

PAT: They've lost their brother. You know what that means, Dick.
Nixon sighs, watches the TV – images of a touch football game in Hyannis Port.
SHARP CUT BACK TO:

32. INT. NIXON HOUSE. BEDROOM. DAY (1925).
ARTHUR NIXON (7) *cries in pain.* RICHARD (12) *helps*
FRANK, *his father, hold him on the bed as a*
DOCTOR *twists a long needle into the base of*
Arthur's spine.

ARTHUR: Daddy! Please! Make it STOP!!!
   Arthur's eyes roll onto Richard for help, Richard
   can't bear it, pulls away.

33. INT. NIXON HOUSE. PARLOR. DAY (1925).
FRANK *comes down the narrow stairs, shocked,*
fighting tears. HANNAH *sits reading her Bible. The*
BOYS *linger nervously around their made-up cots in*
the parlor.

FRANK (*sobs*): The doctors are afraid the little darling is
   going to die . . .

34. INT. ARTHUR BEDROOM. DAY.
ARTHUR *laps at some tomato gravy on toast, which*
makes him happy. His face is angelic, as if he were
getting better.
   HANNAH *feeds him, cleans his lips with a napkin, as*
RICHARD *sits close by, squeezing Arthur's hand, puzzled*
by it all. FLASHES *run through his head – Arthur sitting*
on his lap, learning to read; Dick swinging Arthur by his
arms. DON *and* HAROLD *are also there. The Doctor has*
gone.

ARTHUR (*low*): Thank you, Mama, I feel better . . . I'm
  sleepy.

HANNAH (*removing the food*): We'll let thee rest now,
  my little angel.
  *She tucks him in. He yawns. The brothers are
  awkward, ready to leave. Arthur turns his loving
  eyes on Richard.*

ARTHUR: Richard, don't you think . . . I should say a
  prayer before I sleep?
  Richard is awkward, stutters.

HANNAH (*nearly cracking*): Yes, Arthur, I do . . .
  He smiles at her, then:

ARTHUR (*murmurs*): If I should die before I wake, I pray
  the Lord my soul to take . . .
  He slips off, into a coma.
  Richard watches, devastated.

35. INT. NIXON HOUSE. PARLOR. ANOTHER DAY.
RICHARD *runs to his mother,* HANNAH, *who is coming
down the stairs with* FRANK. *She seems very shaken, but
quiet, off in another world. The moment Richard reaches
her, throwing his arms around her skirt, she snaps him
back. A harsh, angry voice.*

HANNAH: No! . . . No. Don't . . .
  *Richard is shocked as his mother sweeps by in her
  private grief.*

74

36. INT. NIXON STUDY. NEW YORK APARTMENT. DAY.
RESUME NIXON – *his face lost in the silence of the memory. The television SOUNDS fade back in alongside* PAT'*s voice.*

   TV IMAGE – LYNDON JOHNSON being sworn in.

NIXON: . . . if I'd been president, they *never* would have killed me.
   Pat is bewildered by the statement.

PAT (O.S.): Dick? Are you going to call?
   He looks at her, absent.

PAT: Bobby?
   He looks back at the TV screen.

NIXON (*quietly*): No . . . I'll go through Lyndon. We'll be invited.
   We flash suddenly to Kennedy's head being blown apart. Then back to JOHNSON as we:
   CUT FORWARD TO:

37.
SUBTITLE READS: 'FIVE YEARS LATER – 1968'
DOCUMENTARY IMAGE – CLOSE on LYNDON
JOHNSON *announcing:*

JOHNSON: . . . accordingly, I shall not seek, and I will not accept, the nomination of my party for another term as your president . . .
   CUT TO:

38. INT. NURSING HOME. DAY.
HANNAH NIXON, *in her seventies*.

REPORTER 1 (*V.O.*): . . . Johnson's withdrawal resurrects Richard Nixon as a strong Republican candidate against the war. His mother, Hannah Nixon, just before her death last year, commented on her son's chances . . .

REPORTER 2 (*off*): Mrs. Nixon, do you think your son will ever return to politics?

HANNAH: I don't think he has a choice. He was always a leader.

REPORTER 2 (*off*): Do you think he'd make a great president, Mrs. Nixon?

HANNAH (*unsmiling*): . . . if he's on God's side, yes . . .

39. EXT. NEW YORK APARTMENT BUILDING. DAY (1968).
REPORTERS flock outside the building as NIXON *and his GROUP exit their car, trying to ignore the press.*

40. INT. NIXON APARTMENT. DAY (1968).
NIXON *enters, ebullient, with* MITCHELL, HALDEMAN, ZIEGLER, *taking off their winter coats.*

MITCHELL: Jesus, Dick, never seen anything like it! Even the Goddamn *Times* is saying you got it.

HALDEMAN: Vietnam's gonna put you in there this time, chief.

ZIEGLER: We got the press this time!

NIXON: And we got the 'big mo'! We're back!

PAT (O.S.): So? You've decided?
They turn. PAT *is in the corridor.*

PAT: Were you planning to tell me?

NIXON: We haven't announced anything . . . uh . . .
She's walking away, cold. Dick follows, with a look to his men.

NIXON: Uh, wait . . .

MITCHELL: You need her, Dick – in '60 she was worth five, six million votes.

NIXON: Don't worry – I'll use the old Nixon charm on her.
As he goes:

HALDEMAN (*to the others*): The old Nixon charm? Who could resist that.

41. INT. NIXON BEDROOM. DAY.
NIXON *enters.* PAT *is mechanically taking his identical grey suits from the closet and laying them on the bed.*

NIXON: Buddy? . . .

PAT: You should be going . . . the primaries are soon, aren't they? New Hampshire . . .

NIXON: They love you, Buddy. They need you, too.

PAT: I don't want *them* to love me.

NIXON: I need you out there. It won't be like the last time. The war's crippled the Democrats. I can win . . . We deserve it. Yeah, it's ours Buddy – at last. Nobody knows that better than you. Frank Nixon's boy.
Pat slows her packing. Nixon takes her hand.

NIXON: Remember what Mom said? We're not like other people, we don't choose our way. We can really *change things,* Buddy. We've got a chance to get it right. We can change America!
She stops, looks at him, feels his surge of power.

NIXON: It was our dream too, Buddy, together . . . always.

PAT: Do you really want this, Dick?

NIXON: This. Above all.

PAT: And then you'll be happy?
The briefest smile opens her face. He takes the inch, presses in, hugs her.

NIXON: Yes . . . you know it! Yes . . . I will. Yeah!

PAT (*in his embrace*): Then I'll be there for you.

NIXON (*exultant*): You're the strongest woman I ever met. I love you, Buddy.

PAT: Can I just ask for one thing?

NIXON: Anything.

PAT: Will you . . . would you kiss me?
He does so with all the earnestness he is capable of.

42. INT. TELEVISION STUDIO. DAY (1968).
NIXON, *fielding questions, is on a small stage, surrounded by a STUDIO AUDIENCE in a semi-circle. A mike is around his neck, no separation from the people. PAT sits behind him, a campaign smile painted on. Nixon is visible to us on TV monitors inside an engineer's booth.*

NIXON (*on TV*): I would never question Senator Kennedy's patriotism. But going around the country promising *peace at any price* is *exactly* what the North Vietnamese want to hear!
Cheers, applause.

HALDEMAN (*to the TV director*): Cue the crowd. Go to the women's group. Get the bald guy, he's great . . .

NIXON (*TV*): I, unlike Senator Kennedy, have a *plan* to end the war. But not for peace at any price, but *peace with honor!*
INTERCUT:

79

43. EXT. LA COSTA COUNTRY CLUB. ESTABLISHING. DAY.

44. EXT. PRIVATE PATIO. LA COSTA COUNTRY CLUB. DAY.
J. EDGAR HOOVER (60's), *short and fat, covered with steam-room sweat, looks like a Roman emperor, as he watches the television intermittently, taking pictures of* CLYDE TOLSON (50's), *his long-time friend and associate. Tolson has a towel around his waist and one over his head.*

CLYDE (*sarcastic*): What do you think this plan is, Edgar? A nuclear attack?

HOOVER: He's lying, Clyde. Always has. That's why Nixon's always been useful. Hold still. And take your hand off your hip.
JOAQUIN, *a very young, near-naked Hispanic boy, comes in with refreshments: orange slices, fruit, and pastel drinks with parasols.*
INTERCUT TO:

45. INT. TV STUDIO. DAY.
RON ZIEGLER *checks his scripts as* NIXON *continues on the other side of the glass.*

DIRECTOR (*turns*): Who's next?

ZIEGLER: The Negro. We gotta have a Negro.
A BLACK MAN *appears on the monitors.*

BLACK MAN: Mr. Nixon . . . (*Nixon:* '*Yes, sir*') You've

made a career out of smearing people as Communists. And now you're building your campaign on the divisions in this country. Stirring up hatred, turning people against each other . . .
Ziegler and HALDEMAN *are apoplectic.*

HALDEMAN: What the *fuck's* he doing? He's making a speech.

ZIEGLER: Cut him off!

DIRECTOR: I can't cut him off! This isn't Russia!
The Black Man turns to the studio audience.

BLACK MAN: You don't want a real dialogue with the American people. This whole thing's been staged. These aren't real people. You're just a mouthpiece for an agenda that is hidden from us.

HALDEMAN *(screaming)*: Go to commercial!

DIRECTOR: There are no commercials. You bought the whole half hour, baby . . .
The Black Man is walking down the aisle toward Nixon.

BLACK MAN *(impassioned)*: When are you going to tell us what you really stand for? When are you going to take the mask off and show us who you really are?
Close on Nixon's upper lip, sweating.
Haldeman watches intently.

HALDEMAN: It's a high, hard one, chief. Park it.
Nixon gathers himself, looks firmly at the Black Man.

NIXON: Yes, there are divisions in this country (*Black Man: 'Who made them – you made them!'*) . . . but I didn't create them. The *Democrats did!* If it's dialogue you want, you're more likely to get it from me than from the people who are burning down the cities! Just think about that . . . The great Doctor King said the same things. You know, young man, who a great hero is – Abraham Lincoln. Because he stood for common ground, he brought this country together . . .
The audience applauds. Haldeman punches Ziegler's arm.

HALDEMAN: I love that man! I love him. *(then)* Fire the sonofabitch who let that agitator in!

ZIEGLER *(relieved)*: Okay, go to the little girl. Can he see the little girl?

DIRECTOR: She's right down front.

NIXON: I don't know if you can see her, but there's a little girl sitting down here with a sign. Could you hold that up, sweetheart?

ZIEGLER: Bag the guy. Take the sign!
The Camera cuts to a LITTLE GIRL holding a hand-lettered sign.

NIXON: The sign has on it three simple words. 'Bring-us-together!' That is what I want, and that is what the great silent majority of Americans want!
The audience loves it. APPLAUSE signs light up.

NIXON (*shouts over*): And that's why I want to be
   president. I want to bring us together!

46. EXT. PATIO. LA COSTA COUNTRY CLUB. DAY.
Like a lizard, HOOVER *eyes* JOAQUIN, *the Hispanic boy.*

TOLSON: . . . give me a break, Mary.

NIXON (*V.O.: continues*): You all know me. I'm one of
   you. I grew up a stone's throw from here on a little
   lemon ranch in Yorba Linda . . .

HOOVER (*mimics*): It was the poorest lemon ranch in
   California, I can tell you that. My father sold it
   before they found oil on it.

NIXON (*V.O.*): It was the poorest lemon ranch in
   California, I can assure you. My father sold it before
   they found oil on it.

TOLSON (*mimics*): But it was all we had.

NIXON (*V.O.*): . . . but it was all we had.

HOOVER: You're new. What's your name?

JOAQUIN: Joaquin, Mr. Hoover.
   *Hoover selects an orange slice, puts one end between
   his teeth. Wiggles it. Joaquin bends over, bites off
   the other end. Tolson looks peeved.*

NIXON (*V.O.*): My father built the house where I was
   born with his own hands. Oh, it wasn't a big
   house . . .

HOOVER: Turn this crap off, Clyde. It's giving me a headache . . . You may go, Joaquin.
He takes a drink off Joaquin's tray as Clyde turns off the TV. Joaquin vanishes.

HOOVER: I want to see him tomorrow, Clyde.

CLYDE: Edgar, think twice. He works in the kitchen.

HOOVER: Not Joaquin, you idiot. Nixon. Did you hear what he said in Oregon? About me having too much power.

CLYDE: It's between Nixon and a Kennedy again, Edgar . . . Who do you want?

HOOVER: Kennedy – never. He'll fry in hell for what he did to me. But Nixon don't know that, which is why I'm gonna have to remind him he needs us a helluva lot more'n we need him.

47. EXT. DEL MAR RACETRACK. STARTING GATE. DAY.
THOROUGHBREDS explode out of the chutes.

48. EXT. DEL MAR RACETRACK. CLUBHOUSE. DAY.
A private box just above the finish line. HOOVER *raises his binoculars, watching the race. He is wearing a white tropical suit, Panama hat, white shoes.* CLYDE *is dressed similarly.*

JOHNNY ROSELLI, *white hair, deep tan, sharp dresser, sits with him in the box, spots someone . . .*

ROSELLI: Your boy's on the way up . . . I met him years
ago. In Havana.
*ON THE TRACK: TWO HORSES are in a terrific
stretch drive.*
HOOVER *watches impassively.*

ANNOUNCER (O.S.: *frantic*): And down the stretch they
come. It's Sunday's Chance Son and Olly's Boy
dueling for the lead . . .
*CLOSE: OLLY'S BOY puts a nose in front of
SUNDAY'S CHANCE*

HOOVER: He's folding, Johnny.
*ON THE TRACK: Sunday's Chance is tiring, falling
behind Olly's Boy.*

ROSELLI: You just wait a second.
*CLOSE: On Olly's Boy's bandaged front legs. Then,
Olly's Boy's right foreleg snaps. It sounds like a rifle
shot.*
*Olly's Boy goes down over his shoulder. The
JOCKEY is thrown across the track.*
*The CROWD is stunned. Sunday's Chance wins
easily.*
Hoover turns to Roselli.

TOLSON: A bit extreme, isn't it?

ROSELLI: It's the drama. *(gestures to the crowd)* The
crowd loves that shit. Hey! There's Randolph Scott.
You might like that guy, friend of mine. Wanna meet
him, Edgar?
SHOUTING and CHEERS behind them. They turn.

NIXON *is making his way down the aisle, waving to the crowd. He is followed by* HALDEMAN.
Hoover passes Roselli a ticket.

HOOVER: Not now, Johnny. Cash this for me, would you?

ROSELLI: It's a two-dollar bet, Edgar. You got thousands coming on this . . . what the fuck?

HOOVER: I told you, just cash it, Johnny. And don't swear around me . . .
A beat. Roselli crosses Nixon, who enters the box.

NIXON: Edgar, wonderful to see you. Clyde . . . hi.

TOLSON: Mr. Nixon . . .

HOOVER: Thank you for coming, Dick.

NIXON: Winning?

HOOVER: Actually, I've just had a bit of luck.

ANNOUNCER (O.S.): The management of Del Mar is saddened to announce that Olly's Boy will have to be destroyed . . .
Groans from the crowd.

NIXON: Oh, my goodness . . .

HOOVER: How about you? Are you going to win?

NIXON: You should ask Bobby.

TOLSON (*sarcastic*): . . . little Bobby.

HOOVER: Would you walk with me down to the

paddock? I'd like to look at the horses for the eighth.

NIXON: Can't we just talk here? I've got the police chiefs in San Diego.
Hoover moves close.

HOOVER (*whispers*): I'm trying to spare you an embarrassment. Johnny Roselli is on his way back here.
Nixon looks sick.

NIXON: Roselli? Johnny Roselli?

HOOVER: Yes. Your old friend from Cuba.

NIXON: I never met the man.

HOOVER: I know you've been very careful not to. That's why I'm concerned.
Nixon glances at Hoover. Hoover smiles.

49. EXT. DEL MAR RACETRACK. PADDOCK. DAY (1968).
Moving with NIXON, HOOVER *and* TOLSON *along the rail outside the walking ring. FBI AGENTS have cleared a circle around them. The HORSES for the next race are being saddled. Nixon waves and smiles to PATRONS of the track.*

HOOVER: You'll win the nomination.

NIXON: It could be '60 all over again, Edgar. Bobby's got the magic, like a Goddamn rock star. They climb all over each other just to touch his clothes! He'll ride his brother's corpse right into the White House.

TOLSON: Ummm . . .

HOOVER (*nods*): If things remain as they are . . . He's got the anti-war vote.

NIXON: Or he'll *steal* it like his brother. He's a mean little sonofabitch, Edgar . . . He had the IRS audit my *mother* when she was dying in the nursing home . . .

HOOVER: I know . . .

TOLSON (*casually*): . . . Somebody should shoot the little bastard.

NIXON: I wanna fight just as dirty as he does.

TOLSON: . . . Use his women.

NIXON: . . . Any information you have, Edgar. The sonofabitch is not gonna steal from me again! Can you back me up on this? Can I count on your support?

HOOVER (*amused*): I look at it from the point of view that the system can only take so much abuse. It adjusts itself eventually, but at times there are . . . savage outbursts. The late 'Doctor' King for example. A moral hypocrite screwing women like a degenerate tomcat, stirring up the blacks, preaching against our system . . . (*shakes his head*) Sometimes the system comes close to cracking.
Hoover stops in front of a huge GELDING, pats his muzzle.

HOOVER: We've already had one radical in the White House. I don't think we could survive another. *Nixon feels uncomfortable. Images, vague, disturbing. Even the nostrils on the horse seem to be emitting a devil's fire, and the noises of the snorting animal magnify . . .*

NIXON (*a beat*): Yeah, well, as I said, Edgar . . .

HOOVER (*precisely*): You *asked* if you could count on my support . . . As long as I can count on yours.

NIXON (*V.O.: on tape*): The old queen did it on purpose.

50. INT. THE WHITE HOUSE. LINCOLN SITTING ROOM. NIGHT (1973).
RESUME SCENE – NIXON *listens as the tape rolls.*

NIXON (*on tape*): He wasn't protecting me. He was putting me on notice.

HALDEMAN (*on tape*): What? That he knew Johnny Roselli? Hoover knew a lot of gangsters.

NIXON (*on tape*): Yeah, but Roselli wasn't just any gangster. He was the gangster who set up Track 2 in Cuba.

51. INT. EXEC OFFICE BLDG. PRESIDENT'S OFFICE. NIGHT (1972).
NIXON *and* HALDEMAN *are alone. The lights are on.*

Nixon's had a couple of drinks. The talk is a little looser.

HALDEMAN (*confused*): I don't understand. Track 2's Chile?

NIXON: Chile, Congo, Guatemala, Cuba. Wherever there's a need for an Executive Action capability, there's a Track 2. In Cuba, Track 1 was the Bay of Pigs invasion. Track 2 . . . it was our idea. (*stands*) We felt the invasion wouldn't work unless we got rid of Castro. So we asked ourselves – who else wants Castro dead? The Mafia, the money people. So we put together Track 2 . . .
CUBA MONTAGE
Images begin to project from that long-ago time. A YOUNGER NIXON. Macho Cuban 'FREEDOM FIGHTERS' in the Keys and Guatemala. The CIA, the MOB – including JOHNNY ROSELLI. FAT CATS and CASINO BOSSES shaking hands with young Nixon on his visit in the 40's. A Rum and Coca-Cola SONG plays.

NIXON (*softly*): The first assassination attempt was in '60, just before the election.

HALDEMAN (*stunned*): Before?! Eisenhower approved that?

NIXON: He didn't veto it. (*then*) I ran the White House side. The mob contact was Johnny Roselli. (*then*) One of the CIA guys was that jackass, Howard Hunt.

HALDEMAN: Jesus!

NIXON: And not just Hunt. Frank Sturgis, all those Cubans. All of them in the Watergate. They were involved in Track 2 in Cuba. *(then)* Hunt reported to my military aide. But I met with him several times as Vice President. That's what worries the shit out of me. I don't know how much Hunt knows. Or the Cubans.

HALDEMAN: So? You wanted Castro dead. *Everybody* wanted Castro dead. If Hunt and the others are CIA, why don't we just throw this back in the CIA's lap? Let Richard Helms take the fall?

NIXON *(pause)*: Because . . . because Dick Helms knows too much . . . If anyone in this country knows more than I do, it's Hoover and *Helms!* You don't *fuck* with Dick Helms! Period . . .
Pause.

HALDEMAN: Alright. But why, if Kennedy is so clean in all this, didn't *he* cancel Track 2?

NIXON: Because he didn't even know about it. The CIA never told him, they just kept it going. It was like . . . it had a life of its own. Like a kind of 'beast' that doesn't even know it exists. It just eats people when it doesn't need 'em anymore. *(drops back in his chair)* Two days after the Bay of Pigs, Kennedy called me in. He reamed my ass . . .
DOCUMENTARY INTERCUT. Brief, moving, live-action image of JOHN KENNEDY.

NIXON (*continued*): . . . he'd just found out about
   Track 2.

HALDEMAN: You never told him?

NIXON (*softly*): I didn't want him to get the credit. He
   said I'd stabbed him in the back. Called me a two-bit
   grocery clerk from Whittier.
   Nixon's face expresses the deep hurt of that insult.

NIXON: That was the last time I ever saw him.
   *IMAGE – the 'Beast' – an image of Kennedy
   perverted, his head blown off . . .*

HALDEMAN: If they didn't tell Kennedy about Track 2,
   how did Hoover find out?

NIXON: He had us bugged. Christ, he had everybody
   bugged. Yeah, he was gonna support me in '68, but
   he was also threatening me. (*then*) That was Hoover:
   he'd give you the carrot, but he'd make damn sure
   the stick went right up your ass.

52. INT. AMBASSADOR HOTEL. PANTRY (1968).
*DOCUMENTARY FOOTAGE of chaos in the pantry.
The camera is jostled. Women screaming. A man is
being wrestled to the floor.*
   ROBERT KENNEDY lies there, mortally wounded.

NIXON (V.O.): When I saw Bobby lying there on the
   floor, his arm stretched out like that . . .

53. INT. EXECUTIVE OFFICE BLDG. PRESIDENT'S OFFICE.
NIGHT (1973).
RESUME SCENE – NIXON *and* HALDEMAN.

NIXON: . . . his eyes staring . . . *(then)* I knew I'd be
    president. *(beat)* Death paved the way, didn't it?
    Vietnam. The Kennedys. It cleared a path through
    the wilderness for me. Over the bodies . . . Four
    bodies.
    Haldeman corrects him.

HALDEMAN: You mean two . . . two bodies?

54. INT. THE WHITE HOUSE. LINCOLN SITTING ROOM.
NIGHT (1973).

HALDEMAN *(V.O. on tape)*: You mean two . . . two
    bodies?
    RESUME SCENE – NIXON *takes a slug of Scotch,
    then he rubs the bridge of his nose, looks up at the
    portrait of Lincoln. A pause, softly to Mr. Lincoln.*

NIXON *(slurs)*: How many did you have? Hundreds of
    thousands . . . Where would we be without death,
    hunh Abe?
    Nixon stands, steadies himself.

NIXON *(softly)*: Who's helping us? Is it God? Or is it . . .
    Death?
    CUT BACK TO:

55. EXT. SANITARIUM CABIN. PORCH. ARIZONA. DAY (1933).

A lunar landscape — barren, scorched, silent. Suddenly, violent, desperate COUGHING.

HAROLD NIXON *(23) is doubled over the railing, a long string of bloody mucus hanging from his lips. He is shockingly emaciated — the last stages of tuberculosis.* HANNAH NIXON, *in background attending TWO OTHER PATIENTS, looks on at Harold.*

RICHARD *(19) hurries out of the cabin with a cotton cloth. He holds* HAROLD *until he stops heaving. Then, he wipes his mouth.*

HAROLD (*gasps*): . . . that was a whopper.
> *Richard carefully folds the cloth, drops it into a metal container that is already full of them. He stands there, helpless, a solemn boy.*

HAROLD (*panting*): Hey . . . you'll be able to do it now.

RICHARD: What . . .?

HAROLD: Go to law school. Mom and Dad'll be able to afford it now. . . .
> *Richard looks at him in horror.*

HAROLD: Mom expects great things from you . . .

RICHARD: Harold . . . can I get you anything?
> *Harold throws a loving arm around Richard, who tenses. We sense that Harold in some way could have helped Richard, taught him to laugh a bit.*

HAROLD (*a gentle smile*): Relax, Dick, it's just me . . .

The desert's so beautiful, isn't it? *(then)* I want to go home, Dick. Time to go home.

RICHARD *(stiffly)*: You're not gonna quit on me, are you, Harold?
Harold looks out over the landscape. Silence.

56. INT. NIXON HOUSE. PARLOR. NIGHT (1933).
RICHARD *sits staring into the fire. He still wears his black suit from Harold's funeral.* HANNAH *enters quietly.*

HANNAH: Richard?
He looks up at her.

RICHARD: I can't . . .

HANNAH: Thou must.
She moves closer. Casting a shadow over his face.

HANNAH: It's a gift, Richard. This law school is a gift from your brother.

RICHARD *(bitter)*: Did he have to *die* for me to get it?!

HANNAH: It's meant to make us stronger. *(kneels)* Thou art stronger than Harold . . . stronger than Arthur. God has chosen thee to survive . . .

RICHARD: What about happiness, Mother?

HANNAH: Thou must find thy peace at the center, Richard. Strength in this life. Happiness in the next.
DISSOLVE TO:

57. INT. REPUBLICAN CONVENTION. NIGHT (1968).
ON RICHARD NIXON (55) – *in his prime. A profile of his face – as the vast crowd goes berserk. Nixon absorbs the adoration: at last, he has arrived. He looks down at someone in the audience. Points, smiles, waves.*

Then he steps forward, thrusts his arms in the air – the twin-V salute. The cheers rattle the hall as PAT *and their DAUGHTERS join him, followed by Vice President* SPIRO AGNEW *and his FAMILY. Nixon puts his arm around Pat. She waves. The crowd is on its feet.*

NIXON (*privately to Pat*): Now tell me you didn't want this, Buddy.
  Pat smiles back at him, caught up in it. Then she kisses him on the cheek.
  TIME CUT TO:
  NIXON *addresses the DELEGATES (a composite of Nixon speeches).*

NIXON: It's time for some honest talk about the problem of law and order in the United States. I pledge to you that the current wave of violence will not be the wave of the future! (*vast APPLAUSE*)
  INTERCUT WITH:
  DOCUMENTARY FOOTAGE – 1. Civil war.
  Tanks in the streets of DETROIT 2. A BLACK PANTHER safe-house in flames surrounded by FBI AGENTS.

NIXON (V.O.): . . . The long dark night for America is about to end . . . Let us begin by committing ourselves to the truth – to find the truth, to speak the truth. And to live the truth . . . A new voice is being heard across America today: it is not the voice of the protestors or the shouters, it is the voice of a majority of Americans who have been quiet Americans over the past few years . . . a silent majority.

DOCUMENTARY FOOTAGE – 3. GEORGE WALLACE whips a DIXIE CROWD into a frenzy. 4. The WOUNDED KNEE SIEGE is under way – FBI AGENTS and LOCAL MILITANTS pour fire in on the INDIAN MILITANTS. 5. The YIPPIE DEMONSTRATORS outside the CHICAGO DEMOCRATIC CONVENTION. Chicago POLICE wade in with nightsticks, tear gas.

NIXON (*at the podium*): Who are they? Let me tell you who they are – they're in this audience by the thousands, they're the workers of America, they're white Americans and black Americans . . .
We cut among the DELEGATES, seeking to show the face of a populace that is torn by civil war.

NIXON (*cont'd*): . . . they are Mexican Americans and Italian Americans, they're the great silent majority, and they have become angry, finally; angry not with hate but angry, my friends, *because they love America and they don't like what's happened to America these last four years!* We will regain respect for America in the world. A burned American library, a desecrated flag . . . Let us understand: North Vietnam cannot defeat or humiliate the

97

United States. Only Americans can do that!
This brings the house down! As we:
CROSSCUT TO:
DOCUMENTARY FOOTAGE – 6. CHICAGO is
now a full-scale POLICE RIOT. The COPS have lost
all control, swinging nightsticks wildly, breaking
heads, dozens of arrests.
Closing on NIXON at the podium.

NIXON: Let's face it. Most Americans today, in a crisis
of spirit, are simply fed up with government at all
levels. All the Great Society activists are lying out
there in wait, poised to get you if you try to come
after them: the professional welfareists, the urban
planners, the day-carers, the public housers. The
costly current welfare system is a mess, and we are
on the brink of a revolt of the lower middle class.
The bottom line is – no work, no welfare. Our
opponents have exaggerated and over-emphasized
society as the cause of crimes. The war on poverty is
not a war on crime, and it is no substitute for a war
on crime. *(pause)* I say to you, tonight we must have
a new feeling of responsibility, of self-discipline. We
must look to renew state and local government! We
must have a complete reform of a big, bloated
federal government. The average American is just
like the child in the family. You give him some
responsibility and he is going to amount to
something. If you make him completely dependent
and pamper him, you are going to make him soft,
and a very weak individual.

NIXON (*cont'd*): I begin with the proposition that
freedom of choice in housing, education, and jobs is
the right of every American. A good job is as basic a
civil right as a good education. On the other hand, I
am convinced that while legal segregation is totally
wrong, forced integration of housing or education is
just as wrong! We simply have to face the hard fact
that the law cannot go beyond what the people are
willing to support. This was true as far as
Prohibition was concerned. It is far more true with
regard to education and housing . . . Yet those of us
in public service know – we can have full prosperity
in peacetime . . . Yes, we can cut the defense budget.
We can reduce conventional forces in Europe. We
can restore the national environment. We can
improve health care and make it available more
fairly to all people. And yes, we can have a complete
reform of this government. We can have a new
American Revolution.
CROSSCUT TO:
*DOCUMENTARY FOOTAGE – 7. The young
CHICAGO DEMONSTRATORS are chanting
rebelliously at POLICE.*

DEMONSTRATORS: The whole world is watching! The
whole world is watching!
*DOCUMENTARY FOOTAGE – 8. A B-52 unloads
BOMBS and NAPALM over jungle.
SUBTITLE READS: 'LAOS – SECRET BOMBING
CAMPAIGN, 1969-70; 242,000 MISSIONS.'
CUT TO:*

58.
OMIT #58

59. EXT. THE WHITE HOUSE. NIGHT.
The lights are blazing late with war talk.

60. INT. SIDE OFFICE. THE WHITE HOUSE. NIGHT.
In a small paneled room, the talk is angry: BILL ROGERS,
Secretary of State, MEL LAIRD, *Defense Secretary, to one
side;* KISSINGER *with* HAIG, *seen earlier, but now
Kissinger's assistant, to the other side of the desk, as*
NIXON *listens;* HALDEMAN *takes notes.* ZIEGLER *looks
on. Though a stand-up chart displays a large map of
Cambodia's border with South Vietnam, we may note
there are no military personnel in the room.*

ROGERS: . . . It'd be a disaster for us, Mr. President.
    There's a lot of sympathy out there for Cambodia, a
    tiny, neutral Buddhist nation. There'd be protests in
    the streets, right out on your front lawn . . .

LAIRD: . . . Building this Cambodian army up will be
    harder even than the Vietnamese army. They have
    no tradition of . . . The government there would
    collapse if we . . .
    Nixon's eyes narrow, furious.

NIXON: So you're saying, 'Do nothing' – that's what
    you're saying. The same old shit. Well, that's not
    good enough. I'm sick of being pushed around by the

Vietnamese like some pitiful giant. They're using our POWS to humiliate us. What we need now is a bold move into Cambodia; go right after the VC base camps, make 'em scream. That's what I think. You, Henry?

A pivotal moment for Henry. Nixon is clearly scrutinizing Kissinger, who glances at his rivals.

KISSINGER: Well, as you know, most of my staff have weighed in against this 'incursion.' They believe it will fail to achieve anything fundamental militarily, and will result in crushing criticism domestically . . .

NIXON (*interrupts*): I didn't ask what your staff thinks, Henry. What do you think?

KISSINGER (*pause*): What I think is . . . they're *cowards*. Their opposition represents the cowardice of the Eastern Establishment. They don't realize as you do, Mr. President, that the Communists only respect strength, and they will only negotiate in good faith if they fear the 'madman,' Richard Nixon.

Nixon lets a dark smile curl one side of his mouth.

NIXON: *Exactly!* We've got to take the war to them. Hit 'em where it hurts – right in the *nuts*. More assassinations, more killings. Right, Al?

HAIG: That's what they're doing.

NIXON: These State Department jerks, Bill, don't understand; you got to electrify people with bold moves. Bold moves make history, like Teddy

Roosevelt – 'T.R.' – rushing up San Juan Hill. Small event but dramatic. People took notice.

ROGERS: They'll take notice all right.

NIXON: The fact is if we sneak out of this war, there'll be another one a mile down the road. *(pause)* We bite the bullet here. In Cambodia. We blow the hell out of these people!

ZIEGLER: So what should we tell the press?

61.
DOCUMENTARY FOOTAGE – 9. Bombs dropping over Cambodia.

   DOCUMENTARY FOOTAGE – 10. Combined U.S. and SOUTH VIETNAMESE TROOPS invade CAMBODIA.

   SUBTITLE reads: 'APRIL 1970'

NIXON *(V.O.)*: Tonight, American and South Vietnamese units will attack the headquarters for the entire Communist military operation in South Vietnam. *This is not an invasion of Cambodia.* We take this action not for the purpose of expanding the war into Cambodia, but for the purpose of ending the war in Vietnam . . .
CROSSCUT TO:
DOCUMENTARY FOOTAGE – 11. The Administration Building at BERKELEY is burning. POLICE in riot gear move in. A BATTLE between STUDENTS and POLICE is taking place.

REPORTER (*V.O.*): Across the country, several hundred universities are in turmoil as students battle police in protest against the invasion of Cambodia . . .
CUT TO:
DOCUMENTARY FOOTAGE – 11. KENT STATE UNIVERSITY – (1970) A phalanx of NATIONAL GUARDSMEN advances. They look very young and scared. A CROWD of STUDENTS taunts them.

NIXON (*V.O.: a speech*): When I think of those kids out there. Kids who are just doing their duty . . . . . .
CROSSCUT TO:

62. INT. THE WHITE HOUSE. EAST ROOM. DAY.
The end of a ceremony for a released VIETNAM POW.
NIXON, *with* JULIE, *stands before emotional WIVES, DEFENSE DEPARTMENT EMPLOYEES, and UNIFORMED OFFICERS. The POW sits in a wheelchair at Nixon's elbow, emaciated, the blue ribbon of the CMH around his neck.* PAT *is also there.*

NIXON (*continues*): I'm sure they're scared. I was when I was there. But when it really comes down to it . . . *(turns to the POW)* . . . you have to look up to these men. They're the greatest!
Applause. The POW manages a smile.
DOCUMENTARY FOOTAGE – An ugly stand-off. The STUDENTS confront the GUARDSMEN, jeering. The GUARDSMEN lower their bayonets.

STUDENTS (*chanting*): One-two-three-four. We don't
    want your fucking war.
    Someone throws a rock.
    BACK TO SCENE:

NIXON (*continues*): You see these bums, you know,
    blowing up the campuses, burning books and so
    forth. They call themselves 'flower children.' Well, I
    call them spoiled rotten. And I tell you what would
    cure them – a good old-fashioned trip to my Ohio
    father's woodshed. That's what these bums need!
    DOCUMENTARY FOOTAGE – More STUDENTS
    are throwing rocks. The GUARDSMEN are
    momentarily panicked, confused.
    Then, suddenly: they open fire. A melee. Screaming.
    STUDENTS running.
    Then: half a dozen BODIES lie on the ground. A
    young WOMAN crouches over a BODY, crying.

REPORTER I (V.O.): Today, less than twenty-four hours
    after President Nixon called them 'bums,' four
    students were shot dead at Kent State University in
    Ohio.

63. EXT. POTOMAC RIVER. YACHT SEQUOIA. NIGHT.
NIXON *sits at the head of an outdoor dinner table with*
HALDEMAN, EHRLICHMAN, ZIEGLER, KISSINGER. *They*
are being served steaks by MANOLO, *Nixon's Cuban*
valet.

REPORTER I (V.O.): Enraged student groups across the

country are calling for a general strike tomorrow to shut down the *entire* university system until the Vietnam War is ended.

MITCHELL *joins them.*

NIXON (*grim*): How many?

MITCHELL: Four. Two boys. Two girls. And eight wounded.

NIXON: Jesus Christ!

MITCHELL: One of the fathers was on TV saying, 'My child was not a bum.' And it's playing like gangbusters. Hell, Hoover told me one of the girls was a nymph.

NIXON: Shit, the press doesn't care about the facts. Cronkite's sticking it to me. It's their first big hit on Richard Nixon.

ZIEGLER: The governor says they were rioting.

EHRLICHMAN: The governor's full of shit. Most of them were changing classes.

NIXON: Oh, I suppose you would've just let them take over. These aren't fraternity pranks, John. It's anarchy. A revolution!

EHRLICHMAN: I don't know if I'd go that far, sir.

NIXON: Why not?

EHRLICHMAN: Is the war worth it? Is it worth a one-term presidency? Because I think right now that's what we're looking at.

NIXON: I will not go down as the first American president to lose a war! Going into Cambodia, bombing Hanoi, bombing Laos – it buys us time so we can get out and give the South Vietnamese a fighting chance.

KISSINGER: Exactly, sir. That is your historical contribution: to lead boldly in an era of limits.

NIXON (*drinks*): No one understands! – even my own men. What do you think the Communists respond to? Honesty, liberal guilt, soul-wringing crap, fathers on TV crying? Hell no! I understand the Communist mind, I've studied it for thirty years. They grasp 'realpolitik' better than any of us, right, Henry? (*Henry nods*). We gotta make 'em think we're just as tough as they are – that Nixon's a mad bomber, he might do *anything!* I played a lot of poker in World War II (Haldeman and Ehrlichman know the story), and I won big, and let me tell you this – unpredictability is our best asset. That redneck, Johnson, left me a shitty hand and I'm bluffing. I've got to play the hawk in Vietnam and the dove in China. And if we keep our heads, we can win this thing.

ZIEGLER: What? Win Vietnam, sir?

ALL: No . . .

NIXON: No! But what we can do with Vietnam, Ron, is

drive a *stake* through the heart of the Communist alliance! Henry's already getting strong signals from the Chinese. They hate the Viets more than the Russians, and they're worried about a unified Vietnam. The Russians hate the Chinese and are supporting the Viets, you understand? If we stick it out in Vietnam . . . we'll end up negotiating separately with both the Chinese *and* the Soviets. And we'll get better deals than we ever dreamed of from *both* . . . *(Kissinger nods)* That's triangular diplomacy, gentlemen.

KISSINGER: Exactly, yes, Mr. President. That is my contention.

NIXON: That's what geopolitics is *about* – the *whole world linked* by self-interest . . . You tell me, Ron, how the hell I can explain *that* on television to a bunch of simple-minded reporters and weeping fucking mothers!

ZIEGLER: But what am I telling the press about Kent State?

NIXON: Tell 'em what you like; they'll never understand anyway.

EHRLICHMAN: Excuse me . . . Are you talking about recognizing China, Mr. President? That would cost us our strongest support.

NIXON: No . . . I can do this because I've spent my whole career building anti-Communist credentials.

HALDEMAN: If Johnson or Kennedy'd tried it, they'd have crucified them, and rightfully so!

MITCHELL: It's damned risky, Mr. President. Why don't we wait till the second term?

HALDEMAN: This will get him a second term.

NIXON (*repeats*): This will get me a second term. Damn it, without risk, there's no heroism. There's no history. I, Nixon, was born to do this.

KISSINGER: Mr. President, this cannot be breathed! *Especially* to our secretary of state – that cretin Rogers. . . The Chinese would never trust us again. The *only* way, *I emphasize only way,* to pull this off is in secret.

NIXON (*cackles*): This is a major coup, gentlemen – our own State Department doesn't even know. And if it leaks out of here tonight *(pause, he eyes them)* . . . *Pause. Discomfort.*

HALDEMAN: Well, one way or the other, Kent State is *not good*. We have to get out in front of this thing. The PR is going to murder us.

NIXON: Money. Follow the money. *(Haldeman: 'Sir?')* These kids are being manipulated by the Communists. Like Chambers and Hiss.

MITCHELL (*smoking his pipe*): This isn't '48, Dick. They'll never buy it.

NIXON (*angry*): How do you know that, John? Did we

try? Are we just giving up like the rest of 'em. What's Hoover found, for God's sake?

HALDEMAN: Well, he called the other day, sir. He asked for President Harding.
Laughter around the table.

KISSINGER: He's an idiot . . .

HALDEMAN: Seriously, sir, he's gotta go . . .

NIXON: We can't touch Hoover –

EHRLICHMAN: I thought the gloves were off.

NIXON: – as long as he's got secret files on everybody. I don't want 'em used against us. *(frustrated)* What about the CIA?! Helms's done nothing for us. I want to see him.

HALDEMAN: Done.

MITCHELL: With Hiss, Mr. President, you had the microfilm, you had the lie. With the students, we got no proof.

NIXON: The soldiers were provoked. The students started it, for Christ's sake!

EHRLICHMAN: Sir, there's dead American kids here. Let's say we don't apologize for Kent State, but maybe we could have a national prayer day . . .

HALDEMAN: . . . never complain, never explain, John . . .

NIXON (*yells*): I tell you, the soldiers were *provoked*.
Now stop this pussyfooting around. (*irritated*) Dead
kids! How the hell did we ever give the Democrats a
weapon like this? (*then*) I mean, if Cambodia doesn't
work, we'll bomb Hanoi if we have to.
They all look at him. He is resolute.

NIXON: That's right! And if necessary, I'll drop the big
one.

KISSINGER: We have to entertain the possibility . . .
*Nixon looks down at his steak. It is oozing blood.
Too much blood – something is very wrong. He
shoots back, momentarily terrified.*

NIXON: Goddamn it! Who the hell cooked this steak?
(*yells*) Manolo, there's blood all over my plate!
*Nixon throws down his knife and fork and walks
off.*

64. EXT. YACHT SEQUOIA. NIGHT (LATER).
NIXON *is on the bow, alone, watching the city slip by.*
MITCHELL *slides up beside him, offering him a freshened
drink.*

MITCHELL: You all right?

NIXON: My brother Harold was about the same age as
those kids, John. Tuberculosis got him.

MITCHELL: It wasn't your fault. The soldiers were just
kids, too. They panicked.

NIXON: They were throwing *rocks*, John, just rocks. They don't think I feel . . . but I feel too much sometimes. I just can't let a whole policy get dominated by our sentimentality.

MITCHELL: You're doing the right thing, Dick . . . don't let 'em shake you.

NIXON: It broke my heart when Harold died.

MITCHELL: That was a long time ago.
Nixon looks out at the water.

NIXON: I think that's when it starts. When you're a kid. The laughs and snubs and slights you get because you're poor or Irish or Jewish or just ugly. But if you're intelligent, and your anger is deep enough and strong enough, you learn you can change these attitudes by excellence, gut performance, while those who have everything are sitting on their fat butts . . . *(then)* But then when you get to the top, you find you can't stop playing the game the way you've always played it because it's a part of you like an arm or a leg. So you're lean and mean and you continue to walk the edge of the precipice, because over the years you've become fascinated by how close you can get without falling . . . I wonder, John, I wonder . . .
Mitchell puts his hand on Dick's shoulder.

MITCHELL: Get off that. That leads nowhere. You should offer condolences to the families of those kids.

NIXON: Sure, I'd like to offer condolences.

He shrugs off Mitchell's hand and walks down the
deck into the shadows.

NIXON: But Nixon can't.

65. INT. LIMOUSINE. THE WHITE HOUSE. DAY
Leaving the WHITE HOUSE, NIXON *looks out at*
ANGRY DEMONSTRATORS *giving him the finger,*
shaking placards – 'IMPEACH NIXON' *(spelled with a*
swastika), 'PEACE NOW.' *With him are* HALDEMAN
and EHRLICHMAN.

HALDEMAN (*with clipboard*): . . . and we've got the
economic guys at five. The Dow lost another 16
points. They're going to want a decision on the
budget. Sir? . . . Are we holding the line on a
balanced budget?

NIXON (*preoccupied*): No . . . a little deficit won't hurt.
Jesus, they're serious. Why're we stopping?

HALDEMAN (*to the driver*): Run 'em over.
The presidential limousine has a difficult time
negotiating its way through the BLOCKADING
BUSES. *A* MAN *with a* NIXON *mask runs up to the*
window and peers in, before being peeled off by
SECRET SERVICE. *It is an ugly, violent scene, but*
Nixon seems to delight in the threat of action. He's
in an upbeat mood.

NIXON: Get that little fucker! Great tackle! Reminds me

of my days at Whittier. Most of these kids are useless.

HALDEMAN: Probably flunking, nothing to do except come down here and meet girls. Henry's out there with them.

NIXON: There's a poison in the upper classes, Bob. They've had it too soft. Too many cars, too many color TVs . . .

HALDEMAN: Don't forget the South, sir, the West. Filled with good football colleges, straight kids. There's more of 'em with you than against you. Not like these mudmutts.

NIXON: It's the parents' fault really.

EHRLICHMAN: Let's not forget they're just kids, they don't vote.

HALDEMAN: It's the fall of the Roman Empire, are you blind? And we're putting fig leaves on the statues . . .

PROTESTOR: Ho, Ho, Ho Chi Minh is going to win!

HALDEMAN: Get that fucker!
A glum moment. Haldeman stares at him. A PROTESTOR waves a Vietcong flag in Nixon's face. He gets pulled off the limo.

NIXON (*exhilarated*): But, hell, this is *nothing* compared to Venezuela. When I was Vice President, Ike sent me down there like a blocking back. They threw rocks, broke out our windows, almost overturned the car. Read *Six Crises*, Bob. Boy, Pat was brave!

HALDEMAN: Yeah, we've got to get our vice president off the golf course and back out there on the college circuit. That's top priority.

EHRLICHMAN: He's in the dumps, sir. Agnew. Every time you have him attack the press, they give it back to him in spades. He's become the most hated man in America.

NIXON (*chuckles*): Yeah, good old Spiro. Well, better him than me. What the hell is he but an insurance policy?

HALDEMAN: We gotta keep reminding those media pricks, if Nixon goes they end up with Agnew. *They all laugh.*

EHRLICHMAN: He's begging for a meeting, chief. He wants to go overseas for a while.

NIXON: Well, no place where they speak English. That way we can always say he was misquoted. (*emits a high, manic laugh*)
The PROTESTORS are frustrated as the limousine breaks through.

66. INT. CIA HEADQUARTERS. LOBBY. DAY (1970).
The SEAL of the CIA: 'You shall know the truth and the truth shall make you free.' We CRANE BACK, revealing

that the seal is on the floor of the LOBBY as NIXON *strides in with his* ENTOURAGE.

LT GENERAL ROBERT CUSHMAN *hurries out, ruffled, to meet* NIXON.

CUSHMAN: Mr. President, I don't know what to say. As soon as we learned from the Secret Service you were en route, the Director was notified. He should be here any minute.

NIXON: Where the hell is he?

CUSHMAN: Uh, he's rushing back from his tennis game, sir . . .

NIXON (*impatient*): So . . . Let's go . . .

CUSHMAN (*walking with Nixon*): He told me to take you to his conference room.

NIXON: No. His office. (*aside*) I want a very private conversation. I don't want to be bugged.

CUSHMAN: Then his office will be fine.

67. INT. OPERATIONS CENTER & HELMS'S OFFICE. DAY.
They walk past ANALYSTS *laboring in isolation behind Plexiglass walls; the hum of computers, a dark austerity to the place. They all glance up as* NIXON *strides past.*

NIXON: How's the job coming, Bob?

CUSHMAN: Frankly sir, it stinks. I have no access. I'm lucky Helms lets me have a staff.

NIXON (*ominous*): We'll see about that . . .

CUSHMAN (*sensing change*): He's nervous, sir. He's heard you're looking for a new director.

NIXON: Well, he certainly isn't acting like it.

CUSHMAN: That's Helms. He's 'sang froid,' a world-class poker player.

NIXON (*under his breath*): Yeah? Well, I own the fucking casino.

68. INT. HELMS'S OFFICE. DAY.
A DUTY OFFICER opens the door of the director's office with a flourish. Nixon catches RICHARD HELMS *throwing his trench coat and tennis racket on a chair, obviously hurrying in from a secret door. Helms spots Nixon, extends his hand with a reptilian smile.*

HELMS: I'm honored, Dick, that you've come all this way out here to Virginia to visit us at last.

NIXON: My friends call me 'Mister President.'

HELMS: And so shall I. *(to Cushman)* Arrange for some coffee, would you General Cushman?
Cushman stares back a beat, bitterly. Nixon signals to Haldeman and Ehrlichman that he, too, wants to be alone. The door closes.

NIXON: Robert Cushman is a lieutenant general in the Marine Corps, the Deputy Director of the CIA . . . and this is what you use him for?

HELMS: I didn't choose him as my deputy, Mr. President. You did.

Nixon paces the office, which is festooned with photos, awards, and an abundance of flowers, particularly orchids. A collector.

NIXON: You live pretty well out here. Now I understand why you want to keep your budgets classified.

Helms sits on a settee, a hard-to-read man.

HELMS: I suppose, 'Mister President,' you're unhappy that we have not implemented your Domestic Intelligence plan, but . . .

NIXON: You're correct. I'm concerned these students are being funded by foreign interests, whether they know it or not. The FBI is worthless in this area. I want your full concentration on this matter . . .

HELMS: Of course we've tried, but so far we've come up with nothing that . . .

NIXON (*stern*): Then find something. And I want these leaks stopped. Jack fucking Anderson, the *New York Times,* the State Department – I want to know who's talking to them.

HELMS: I'm sure you realize this is a very tricky area, Mr. President, given our charter and the congressional oversight committees . . .

NIXON: Screw congressional oversight. I know damn

well, going back to the 50's, this agency reports what
it wants, and buries what it doesn't want Congress
to know. Pay close attention to this.
*Nixon fixes him with his stare. Helms clears his
throat.*

HELMS: Is there something else that's bothering you, Mr.
President?

NIXON: Yes . . . It involves some old and forgotten
papers. Things I signed as Vice President. I want the
originals in my office and I don't want copies
anywhere else.
*Now knowing Nixon's cards, Helms relaxes – about
an inch.*

HELMS: You're referring, of course, to chairing the
Special Operations Group as Vice President.

NIXON: Yes . . .
*Helms wanders over to his prize orchids, fingers
them.*

HELMS: As you know . . . that was unique. Not an
operation as much as . . . an organic phenomenon. It
grew, it changed shape, it developed . . . insatiable,
devouring appetites. (*then*) It's not uncommon in
such cases that things are not committed to paper.
That could be very . . . embarrassing.
*Nixon is embarrassed, and does not like it. Suddenly,
the Beast is in the room.*

HELMS (*reminding him*): I, for one, saw to it that my

118

name was never connected to any of those operations.
On Nixon, waiting.

HELMS (*fishing*): Diem? Trujillo? Lumumba? Guatemala? Cuba? . . . It's a shame you didn't take similar precautions, Dick.

NIXON (*very uncomfortable*): I'm interested in the documents that put your people together with the others. All of them . . .
A beat. This is the fastball. Helms pours himself a coffee.

HELMS: President Kennedy threatened to smash the CIA into a thousand pieces. You could do the same . . .

NIXON: I'm not Jack Kennedy. Your agency is secure.

HELMS (*stirs the coffee*): Not if I give you all the cards . . .

NIXON: I promised the American people peace with honor in Southeast Asia. That could take time – two, maybe three years . . . In the meantime, your agency will continue at current levels of funding.

HELMS (*sips his coffee*): Current levels may not be sufficient.

NIXON: The President would support a reasonable request for an increase.
Helms smiles.

HELMS: And me? . . .

NIXON: Firing you, Mr. Helms, wouldn't do any good. Of course you'll continue as DCI. You're doing a magnificent job.

HELMS: And of course I accept. I'm flattered. And I want you to know, I work for only one president at a time.

NIXON: Yes. And you will give General Cushman full access.

HELMS (*grudgingly accepts that*): It will take a little time, but I'll order a search for your papers. Though it does raise a disturbing issue.

NIXON: What?

HELMS: Mr. Castro.

NIXON (*tense*): Yes.

HELMS: We have recent intelligence that a Soviet nuclear submarine has docked at Cienfuegos.

NIXON: Well, we'll lodge a formal protest.

HELMS: I don't think we can treat this as a formality. Mr. Kennedy made a verbal promise to the Russians not to invade Cuba. But you authorized Dr. Kissinger to put this *in writing*.
Nixon is taken aback by Helms's inside knowledge.

NIXON: Are you tapping Kissinger?

HELMS: My job, unpleasant sometimes, is to know what others don't want me to know.

NIXON (*cold*): Not if you have spies in the White House, it isn't your job.

HELMS: It is not my practice to spy on the president. Doctor Kissinger manages to convey his innermost secrets to the world at large on his own.

NIXON (*absorbs this*): Mr. Helms, we've lived with Communism in Cuba for ten years . . .

HELMS: . . . But it has never been the policy of this government to accept that. And it is certainly not CIA policy.

NIXON: CIA policy? The CIA has no policy, Mr. Helms. Except what I dictate to you . . . (*beat, they stare at each other*) I try to adjust to the world as it is today, not as you or I wanted it to be ten years ago.

HELMS: Is that why you and Kissinger are negotiating with the Chinese?
A beat. Nixon stares.

HELMS: This is an extremely dangerous direction, Mr. President. Terrible consequences can result from such enormous errors of judgment.

NIXON: But . . . if we were able to separate China from Russia once and for all, we can — we could create a balance of power that would secure the peace into the next century.

HELMS: By offering Cuba to the Russians as a consolation prize?

NIXON: Cuba would be a small price to pay.

HELMS: So President Kennedy thought.
A disturbing image suddenly appears in Nixon's mind – KENNEDY with his head blown off in Dallas. Followed by an IMAGE of his own death. In a coffin.
The smell of the orchids in the room is overwhelming. Nixon feels himself dizzy.

NIXON: I never thought Jack was ready for the presidency. But I would never, never consider . . . *(then)* His death was awful, an awful thing for this country. *(then)* Do you ever think of death, Mr. Helms?

HELMS: Flowers are continual reminders of our mortality. Do you appreciate flowers?

NIXON: No. They make me sick. They smell like death . . . I had two brothers die young. But let me tell you, there are worse things than death. There is such a thing as evil.

HELMS: You must be familiar with my favorite poem by Yeats? 'The Second Coming'?

NIXON: No.

HELMS: Black Irishman. Very moving. 'Turning and turning in the widening gyre / The falcon cannot hear the falconer / Things fall apart, the center cannot hold / Mere anarchy is loosed upon the world / And everywhere the ceremony of innocence is drowned / The best lack all conviction, while the worst are full of passionate 'intensity'. . . But it ends so beautifully ominous – 'What rough beast, its hour come round at last / Slouches toward Bethlehem to be born?' . . . Yes, this country stands at such a juncture.

On Nixon, as we CUT TO:

69. INT. THE WHITE HOUSE. NIXON BEDROOM. NIGHT.
NIXON *has just returned from a dinner party, his tuxedo coming off, on the phone, a Scotch in hand, in high spirits. A series of JUMP CUTS of his phone self follows:*

NIXON: It was sudden death, Trini, but I think I kicked Helms's ass. *(laughs)* Yeah, and Kissinger's running around like a scared chicken right now; he doesn't know who's gonna grab his power. Yeah . . . you should see him. I call Haig, Kissinger shits! *(laughs)* JUMP CUT TO:

NIXON (*on phone*): Did you see the look on Hoover's face? He was redder than a beet. That little closet fairy's got no choice. He hates McGovern and Kennedy so much, he's got to love me. And Lyndon? PAT *enters, in a nightdress, smoking.*

PAT: He looked old, didn't he?

NIXON (*hardly noticing*): I asked him, 'Lyndon, what would you do, on a scale of one to ten?' And he said, 'Bomb the shit out of Hanoi, boy! Bomb them where

they live.' . . . John, do you think I was too soft on
TV?
JUMP CUT TO:

NIXON: Bob, I want to get on this energy thing
tomorrow – we really have to rethink our needs to
the end of the century. Let's do it at 1:00. And don't
forget the budget boys. I'm gonna carve the shit out
of 'em. *(beat)* Well, no, clear the afternoon and tell
Trini I'll be in Key Biscayne by 4:00 . . . No, alone . . .
Pat's staying here with the girls.
*Pat approaches, nuzzles him. She seems a little
strange, tipsy . . . but sexy in her nightdress.*

PAT: I'd like to go with you.

HALDEMAN (*O.S.*): Hello?

NIXON (*To Pat*): Uh, you should check with Bob . . . *(to
Bob)* Listen, Bob, I'll call you in the morning.
He hangs up, awkward.

NIXON: Hi, Buddy. What are you doing in here?

PAT: I've missed you.

NIXON (*suspecting drink on her breath*): Are you okay?

PAT: Why don't we go down to Key Biscayne together?
Just the two of us.

NIXON: Because . . . I have to relax.

PAT: I was thinking tonight – do you remember, Dick . . .?

124

Do you remember when you used to drive me on dates with the other boys? You didn't want to let me out of your sight.

NIXON: Yeah, sure, a long time ago.

PAT: Yes, it's been a long time . . . *(a signal given)* *He recoils, embarrassed. A slight sweat.*

NIXON: I don't need that, Buddy. I'm not Jack Kennedy.

PAT *(rebuffed, distant)*: No, you're not. So stop comparing yourself to him. You have no reason to . . . You have everything you ever wanted. You've earned it. Why can't you just enjoy it?

NIXON: I do. I do. In my own way.

PAT: Then what are you scared of, honey?

NIXON: I'm not scared, Buddy. *(a pause)* You don't understand. They're playing for keeps, Buddy. The press, the kids, the liberals – they're out there, trying to figure out how to tear me down.

PAT: They're all your enemies?

NIXON: Yes!

PAT: You personally?

NIXON: Yes! This is about me. Why can't you understand that, you of all people? It's not the war – it's Nixon! They want to destroy Nixon! And if I expose myself even the slightest bit they'll tear my insides out. Do you want that? Do you want to see that, Buddy? It's not pretty.

PAT: Sometimes I think that's what you want.

NIXON: You've been drinking. What the hell are you saying? Jesus, you sound like them now! *(a beat, quietly)* I've gotta keep fighting Buddy, for the *country*. These people running things, the elite . . . they're soft, chickenshit faggots! They don't have the long-term vision anymore. They just want to cover their asses or meet girls or tear each other down. Oh, God, this country's in deep trouble, Buddy . . . and I have to see this through. Mother would've wanted no less of me . . . I'm sorry, Buddy.
Pat stands, about to leave.

PAT: I just wish . . . you knew how much I love you, that's all. It took me a long time to fall in love with you, Dick. But I did. And it doesn't make you happy. You want *them* to love you . . .
Pat waves outward, indicating the world, the public.

NIXON *(interjects)*: No, I don't. I'm not Jack . . .

PAT: But they never will, Dick. No matter how many elections you win, they never will.
She leaves. He is left in the middle of the room. He shuffles to the phone, picks it up.

70. INT. THE WHITE HOUSE. KITCHEN. NIGHT.

NIXON *(V.O.)*: Manolo! Where the hell are you?

126

The lights come on, revealing MANOLO SANCHEZ, *the valet, in the doorway, wearing bathrobe and slippers.*

MANOLO: I was asleep, Mr. President. What can I get you?

NIXON: Just . . . uh . . . you know.

MANOLO: Of course.
Manolo moves to a cabinet on the far side of the pantry. Takes out a bottle of Chivas, puts ice into a tumbler.

NIXON: Do you miss Cuba, Manolo?

MANOLO: Yes, Mr. President.

NIXON: We let you down, didn't we. Your people.

MANOLO: That was Mr. Kennedy.

NIXON: You don't think he was a hero?
Manolo pours Nixon a drink.

MANOLO (*shrugs*): He was a politician.

NIXON (*swallows the drink*): Did you cry when he died?

MANOLO: Yes.

NIXON: Why?

MANOLO: I don't know. (*then*) He made me see the stars . . .

NIXON (*looks outside, to himself*): How did he do that? (*then*) All those kids . . . Why do they hate me so much?

71. EXT. LINCOLN MEMORIAL. PRE-DAWN.
NIXON *gets out of the front of the presidential LIMOUSINE.* MANOLO *follows.*

Nixon looks up: a surreal scene. The Lincoln Memorial has been turned into a pagan temple. FIRES burn on the broad marble steps, half-naked KIDS sleep on filthy blankets below the immense columns. Hendrix plays faintly on a portable radio. Nixon starts up the steps, picking his way among the sleeping forms.

He passes a GIRL, tripping, eyes closed, twirling a long scarf over her head. He stares at her, steps on a sleeping bag.

STUDENT 1: Fuck, man. That's my fuckin' leg –
The boy's jaw drops. Nixon towers over him. An apparition.

NIXON: You just go back to sleep now, young fella.

STUDENT 1 (*rubs his eyes*): Whoa, this is some nasty shit . . .
Nixon reaches the top of the monument. Taped to one of the pillars is a poster: Nixon scowling, and the motto 'Would You Buy A Used Car From This Man?'
Nixon peers at it, moves inside. He looks up at LINCOLN in the eerie firelight. Banners with peace

128

signs have been draped over his shoulders, bunches of flowers between his fingers.
HALF A DOZEN STUDENTS are talking among themselves. They see Nixon, stop. Stunned. Nixon strides toward them.

NIXON: Hi, I'm Dick Nixon.

STUDENT 2: You're shittin' me.

NIXON: Where you from?

STUDENT 2: Syracuse.

NIXON: The Orangemen! Now there's a football program. Jim Brown. And that other tailback . . . The one with the blood disease . . .

STUDENT 2: Ernie Davis.

NIXON: Right, right. I used to play a little ball myself at Whittier. *(laughs nervously)* Of course, they used me as a tackling dummy . . .
A self-possessed YOUNG WOMAN abruptly interrupts.

YOUNG WOMAN: We didn't come here to talk about football. We came here to end the war.

NIXON *(chastened)*: Yes, I understand that.
Pause. Nobody responds.

NIXON: Probably most of you think I'm a real SOB. I know that. But I understand how you feel, I really do. I want peace too, but peace with honor.

STUDENT 3: What does that mean?

NIXON: You can't have peace without a price. Sometimes you have to be willing to fight for peace. And sometimes to die.

STUDENT 3: Tell that to the GIs who are going to die tomorrow in Vietnam.

STUDENT 2: What you have to understand, Mr. Nixon, is that we are willing to die for what we believe in.

NIXON (*looks up at Lincoln*): That man up there lived in similar times. He had chaos and civil war and hatred between the races . . . Sometimes I go to the Lincoln Room at the White House and just pray. You know, the liberals act like idealism belongs to them, but it's not true. My family went Republican because Lincoln freed the slaves. My grandmother was an abolitionist. It was Quakers who founded Whittier, my hometown, to abolish slavery. They were conservative Bible folk, but they had a powerful sense of right and wrong . . . Forty years ago I was looking, as you are now, for answers. (*then*) But you know, ending the war and cleaning up the air and the cities, feeding the poor – my mother used to feed hobos stopping over at our house – none of it is going to satisfy the spiritual hunger we all have, finding a meaning to this life . . .
HALDEMAN *arrives with SEVERAL SECRET SERVICE AGENTS, looking very worried. The crowd around Nixon has grown much larger.*

HALDEMAN: Mr. President!

130

NIXON: It's okay, Bob, we're just rapping, my friends and I. We actually agree on a lot of things . . .

YOUNG WOMAN: No, we don't! You're full of shit! You say you want to end the war, so why don't you? My brother died over there last November. Why? What good was his death?

NIXON: I know. I know. I've seen a lot of kids die too, in World War II.

STUDENT 2: Come on, man – Vietnam ain't Germany. It doesn't threaten us. It's a civil war between Vietnamese.

NIXON: But change always comes slowly. I've withdrawn more than half the troops. I'm trying to cut the military budget for the first time in thirty years. I want an all-volunteer army. But it's also a question of America's credibility, our position in the world . . .

YOUNG WOMAN: You don't want the war. We don't want the war. The Vietnamese don't want the war. So why does it go on?
Nixon hesitates, out of answers.

YOUNG WOMAN: Someone wants it . . . *(a realization)* You can't stop it, can you. Even if you wanted to. Because it's not *you*. It's the system. And the system won't let you stop it . . .

NIXON: There's a lot more at stake here than what you want. Or even what I want . . .

YOUNG WOMAN: Then what's the point? What's the

point of being president? You're powerless.
The girl transfixes him with her eyes. Nixon feels it.
The nausea of the Beast makes him reel. The
students press on him from all sides.

NIXON (*stumbling*): No, no. I'm not powerless. Because
. . . because I understand the system. I believe I can
control it. Maybe not control it totally. But . . . tame
it enough to make it do some good.

YOUNG WOMAN: It sounds like you're talking about a
wild animal.

NIXON: Maybe I am.
A silence. Nixon looks at her.
Haldeman and the SECRET SERVICE MEN fill the
succeeding beat of silence by moving Nixon off. He
allows himself to be herded, waving absently to the
protestors.

HALDEMAN: We really must go, Mr. President.

NIXON (*to all*): Don't forget, the most important thing in
life is your relationship with your Maker . . . (*over*
his shoulder to all) Don't forget to be on God's side.
This doesn't go down well with the protestors.
(*'Bullshit!'*)
As Nixon is led down the steps to the limousine:

NIXON: She got it, Bob. A nineteen-year-old college
kid . . .

HALDEMAN: What?

NIXON: She understood something it's taken me twenty-five fucking years in politics to understand. The CIA, the Mafia, the Wall Street bastards . . .

HALDEMAN: Sir?

NIXON (*climbing into the limo, mutters*): . . . 'The Beast.' A nineteen-year-old kid. She understands the nature of 'the Beast.' She called it a wild animal. *The door closes. The LIMOUSINE is whisked away under searchlights and heavy security.*
SUBTITLE READS: 'JUNE 1971 – A YEAR LATER'
DOCUMENTARY FOOTAGE – The White House is still ringed. ARMED TROOPS patrol Pennsylvania Avenue. The BUSES are drawn up. SMOKE is in the air. The SOUNDS of cherry bombs going off. Signs that read: 'End the war! Throw the fascists out! Dick Nixon before he dicks you.'

72. EXT. THE WHITE HOUSE. ROSE GARDEN. DAY.
Inside the barricades, a fairyland. A white lattice gazebo draped with flowers. TRICIA's wedding is in preparation. GROUNDSKEEPERS and various PERSONNEL lay out the carpet to the altar.

73. INT. EXECUTIVE OFFICE BUILDING. PRESIDENT'S OFFICE. DAY.
J. EDGAR HOOVER joins NIXON, pulling on his wedding tuxedo, at a window, looking out at the PROTESTORS. Intermittently, Hoover helps him with his clothes.

133

NIXON (*musing*): There must be a quarter-million out there, Edgar. They've been at it now for a year. Young kids just like Tricia. I don't know. Do you think they have a point, Edgar? Maybe this whole damned system of government is . . .

HOOVER (*suspecting softness*): Remember what Lenin said in 1917, Mr. President: 'The power was lying in the streets just waiting for someone to pick it up.' The Communists have never been closer. Now is the time to go back to the old themes. The ones that made you president. Let the Communists know you're onto them.

NIXON (*laughs*): The little bastards think they can ruin Tricia's wedding by dancing naked in the Reflecting Pond.

HOOVER: Don't listen to 'em, don't quit. Remember – Kennedy, Bobby, and King were against the war. Where are they now? Don't give 'em a Goddamn inch on the war. President Johnson bombed Laos for years and nobody knew or said a thing. How the hell the *Times* ever got ahold of this Ellsberg stuff is a disgrace!

NIXON: We can't keep a Goddamn secret in this government, Edgar. They're stealing papers right out of this office.

HOOVER: Johnson had the same damned problem till he bugged his own office.

NIXON (*nods*): We took his system out.

HOOVER: That was a mistake. The White House was full of Kennedy people then. It still is.

NIXON: Who do you think is behind it?

HOOVER: Well, you have CIA people all over this place. Helms has seen to that. (*beat, Nixon remains poker-faced*) Then there's Kissinger's staff. Kissinger himself, I believe, may be the leaker.

NIXON (*stunned*): Kissinger?

HOOVER: He's obsessed with his own image. He wants his Nobel Peace Prize a little too much. As the late 'Doctor' King proved – even an ape can win a prize with good press.

NIXON: Jesus, I'd like to book him into a psychiatrist's office. He comes in here ranting and raving, dumping his crap all over the place . . . Could you prove it, Edgar?

HOOVER: I always get my man.

NIXON: Yeah, you do. (*then*) I'd be bugging myself, Edgar . . . Who'd get the tapes?

HOOVER: No one. Your property. It would prove your case. Why do you think Kissinger's taping your calls? For history. His word against yours – and right now he's got the records.
Nixon is stung by the comparison, fussing with his bow tie. Hoover helps him.

NIXON: This damned tie . . . Will you help me, Edgar? (*then*) Churchill used to say to me, 'if you want your own history written properly, you must write it yourself' . . . (*starts out*) All right, Edgar, but just don't let it come back and haunt me.

HOOVER (*a reminder*): It won't. As long as I'm here. *Nixon absentmindedly shows Hoover through a small door into his BATHROOM . . . There is an awkward pause, as both men are too proud to pretend they are cramped in this place together. Hoover clears his throat and exits the regular door. As we hear the Love Theme from 'Doctor Zhivago'. CUT TO:*

74. INT. EAST ROOM. DAY
The White House GUARDS wear German comic opera uniforms including tall cylindrical hats with beaks. We see champagne, white lace, the MUSICIANS wearing morning coats. HOOVER and TOLSON are together, very happy. To the sound of wedding MUSIC, NIXON takes a turn with his daughter, TRICIA, in gown. He has never seemed happier.

NIXON: I am very proud of you today, princess. Very. *When one of the GROOMSMEN cuts in, Nixon asks several OTHERS to dance. He retreats to JULIE's side. Julie says something sweet but unheard to him.*
PAT *is at a window, upset, looking out at the PROTESTORS as Julie comes over to get her.*

JULIE: Come on, Mother, join the . . . *(sees her look)*
     What's the matter?

PAT: We're just not going to buckle to these people.
     Pat puts on her party face and rejoins the crowd.

75. INT. THE WHITE HOUSE. CABINET ROOM. DAY (1971).
RAIN.
*CABINET MEMBERS chat, lean back in their chairs,
smoking, as* NIXON *suddenly erupts into the room, a
focused fury on his face. He sits, slams the* New York
Times *down. CLOSE – we can make out the words
'Pentagon Papers.'*

NIXON: Gentlemen, we've had our last damned leak!
     This is no way to run a Goddamn government.
     We're going to prosecute the hell out of Ellsberg and
     anyone else who wants to leak. And that means any
     one of you who crosses the line, I'm personally going
     after . . .
     INTERCUTTING among the faces – KISSINGER
     *predominant. Nixon glances in his direction, pauses
     on him.*

NIXON: The permissiveness of this era is over. The belts
     are coming off and people are gonna be taken to the
     woodshed. This government cannot survive with a
     counter-government inside it. I know how traitors
     operate – I've dealt with them all my life. This
     bullshit to the effect – some stenographer did it,
     some stenographer – that's never the case. It's never

137

the little people – little people do not leak. It's
always a sonofabitch like Ellsberg who leaks! The
Harvard Hebrew boys with the private agendas who
wanna be heroes.
Nixon grabs the paper, shakes it.

NIXON: Ellsberg did this 'for the good of the country.' I
suppose you've never heard that one before. Alger
Hiss and the Rosenbergs said the same damn crap,
and you know what happened to them – ol' Sparky
got 'em. They've always underestimated Nixon, the
intellectuals. Well, we're gonna let them know we
can fight just as dirty. This is sudden death,
gentlemen. We're gonna get 'em on the ground, stick
in our spikes and twist, show 'em no mercy!
*Nixon looks around the room. The Cabinet
members are stunned.*

NIXON: This administration is a Goddamn disaster. We
got bums out there at the gates. We've got thirty-
eight of forty pieces of our domestic legislation
defeated in Congress. Unless we turn things around,
we'll all be looking for jobs next year. (*then*) Starting
today, nobody in this room talks to the press
without clearing it first with Haldeman. That means
a complete freeze on the *New York Times*, CBS,
Jack fucking Anderson, and the *Washington Post*!
From now on, Haldeman is the Lord High
Executioner. So don't you come whining to me when
he tells you to do something, 'cause that's me
talking. And if you come to me, I'll be tougher than
he is. Anybody tries to screw us, his head comes off.

Do you understand? Good day, gentlemen . . .
He walks out, leaving them stunned and silent.

HALDEMAN: Well, I guess that's it for today's meeting . . .

76. INT. POULTRY PROCESSING PLANT. MIAMI. NIGHT.
*A chicken's head flies off. The CUBAN CROWD is
going crazy as a FIGHTING COCK is moving in for the
kill. The ring is surrounded by impromptu bleachers, the
walls lined with metal cages filled with chickens. The
slaughterhouse is adjacent.*
　HOWARD HUNT *stands at the edge of the crowd,
holding a greasy wrapper of churos, as the fight ends.*
　Cheers and groans. Fistfuls of money are exchanged.
　FRANK STURGIS *turns from the ring, makes his way to
Hunt, hands him a twenty.*

STURGIS: How the fuck did you know?

HUNT: Injections. Even this noble sport's been fixed.
　(pockets the twenty) Seen the guys?

STURGIS: They're around.
　Sturgis snags a piece of churo, swallows it.

STURGIS: Why, you got a customer?

HUNT: The White House.

STURGIS *(stops)*: You're fucking me.

HUNT: We're gonna be plumbers, Frank. We're gonna
　plug leaks.

STURGIS: Who we working for?

HUNT: A guy named Gordon Liddy. Thinks he's Martin Borman. You wanna meet him? (*He motions.*)
GORDON LIDDY *comes out of the edges of the crowd, shakes hands with Sturgis.*

HUNT: Gordon Liddy . . . Frank Sturgis.
They turn the handshake into a parallel of the cock fight, iron grips subtly crushing the other's hand.

LIDDY (*after they break*): Y'ever hold your hand over a fire? (*pulls out a Zippo lighter*)

HUNT: That's okay, Gordon. (*motions him off*)
As Liddy drifts off:

STURGIS: Where'd you find him?

HUNT: Just don't tell him to do anything you don't really want him to do.

STURGIS: So, does Tricky Dick know about this?

HUNT: I won't tell him if you won't.
The HANDLERS throw TWO NEW FIGHTING COCKS into the ring. They start to rip at each other.

HUNT (*chewing on his churo*): The claws are out, Frank.

77. INT. FIELDING PSYCHIATRIST OFFICE. NIGHT (1971).
As seen before: a GLASS shatters, a CROWBAR jacks

open the door marked: 'Dr. Lewis J. Fielding,
Psychiatrist.'

NIXON (V.O.): History will never be the same.
  Cabinets full of pills are overturned. The disguised
  HUNT and LIDDY, with the three CUBANS, go to
  work. A FILE FOLDER is ripped from a cabinet. In
  the flashlight beam the file reads 'Daniel Ellsberg.' A
  VOICE calls out: 'Howard, I got it!'

NIXON (V.O.): We've taken a step into the future. We
  have changed the world.
  'America the Beautiful' MUSIC takes us into:

78. INT. MAO TSE-TUNG'S OFFICE. BEIJING. DAY (1972).
SUBTITLE READS – 'FEBRUARY 1972'
  NIXON *beams, standing under a huge red flag bearing*
the hammer and sickle. The 'America' theme is being
played on traditional Chinese instruments as CHINESE
PHOTOGRAPHERS are allowed to take stiff portraits.
The MEN chit-chat.

NIXON: I must say you look very good, Mr. Chairman.

MAO: Looks can be deceiving . . .

NIXON: We know you've taken a great risk in inviting us
  here.
  MAO *stares at Nixon and replies in Chinese, which*
  the INTERPRETER repeats:

MAO (*half smiles*): I took no risk. I'm too old to be
  afraid of what anyone thinks.

Nixon forces a rigid smile as they move to chairs.
TIME CUT TO:
MAO *and* NIXON *are seated in armchairs opposite each other,* KISSINGER *and* CHOU EN-LAI *to either side of Mao. An* INTERPRETER *between. In media res:*

MAO: Don't ever trust them. They never tell the truth or honor their commitments. Vietnamese are like Russians. Both are dogs.

NIXON (*clears his throat*): Mr. Chairman, there is an old saying: The enemy of my enemy is my friend.

MAO (*smiles*): That has the added virtue of being true. *Mao doesn't seem to be taking any of this too seriously: in fact, he seems a little medicated.*

KISSINGER: You know, Mr. Chairman, at Harvard I used your writings in my class.

MAO: What a waste of time. My writings mean absolutely nothing.

KISSINGER: But your writings have changed the world, Mr. Chairman.

MAO: Fung pi! (*Bullshit!*) I've only managed to change a few things around the city of Beijing. (*then: to Kissinger*) I want to know your secret.

KISSINGER: Secret, Mr. Chairman?

MAO: How a fat man gets so many girls.
Mao howls at his own joke.

KISSINGER: Power, Mr. Chairman, is the ultimate aphrodisiac. *(laughter)*

MAO *(turns to Nixon)*: You know, I voted for you in your last election.

NIXON *(self-effacing)*: I was the lesser of two evils.
A moment. Mao levels a gaze at him, deadly serious.

MAO: You're too modest, Nixon. You're as evil as I am. We're both from poor families. But others pay to feed the hunger in us. In my case, millions of reactionaries. In your case, millions of Vietnamese.

NIXON *(taken aback)*: Civil war is always the cruelest kind of war.

MAO: The real war is in us. *(then)* History is a symptom of our disease.
CUT FORWARD TO:

79.
DOCUMENTARY FOOTAGE – THE BOMBING OF HANOI . . . SUBTITLE READS: 'CHRISTMAS 1972.' HUNDREDS OF B-52 STRIKES, BOMBS POURING OVER THE CITY.

REPORTER *(V.O. BBC accent)*: In a surprise Christmas bombing of Hanoi, President Nixon today delivered more tonnage than was used at Dresden in World War II . . . It is, without doubt, the most brutal bombing in American history.
CROSSCUT:

*DOCUMENTARY FOOTAGE – 1. HANOI – the
devastation of the city. It's on fire. Bodies are
being carried from a collapsed HOSPITAL. 2. The
USA – in contrast, shots in the media of Christmas
trees (Rockefeller Center, etc.); families shopping;
a children's choir singing 'Gloria in Excelsis
Deo.'*

REPORTERS (V.O.): . . . This Christmas bombing has
shaken up the Paris peace talks and created a huge
amount of criticism across the globe. Newspapers
are calling it a 'Stone Age tactic,' and Nixon, a
'maddened tyrant' . . . Nixon's only response: 'When
the Vietnamese take the peace talks seriously, I'll
stop.'
*STOCK FOOTAGE – moving through a bank of
clouds towards the sun.*

80. INT. AIR FORCE ONE. MAIN CABIN. SUNSET (1972).
NIXON *is looking out the window,* PAT *next to him.*
HALDEMAN *and* EHRLICHMAN *are out of earshot.*

PAT: Penny for your thoughts.

NIXON: Is that adjusted for inflation? *(She laughs.)* Think
of the life Mao's led. In '52 I called him a monster.
Now he could be our most important ally. *(then)*
Only Nixon could've done that.

PAT: You're a long way from Whittier.
A beat. He shares her look.

144

NIXON: Yes . . . yes, I am.
Pat puts her hand on his hand.

PAT: Congratulations, Dick.

NIXON (*smiles*): How am I going to break this to Bob
Hope?
KISSINGER *walks into the cabin.*

KISSINGER: We've got the Russians where we want them!
They're calling us. We will have a SALT treaty with
them this year.

HALDEMAN: In time for the election? Brezhnev's tough.
He knows McGovern's right on our ass . . .

KISSINGER: He doesn't have a choice! He has to shift
missiles from Europe to the Chinese border. With
one stroke, the balance of power moves completely
in our favor. This is a coup, Mr. President!

EHRLICHMAN: For you, Henry? Nobel Peace Prize,
maybe . . . (*sees the look on Nixon's face*)

NIXON: Not for the Pentagon it isn't. I'm kissing Mao's
ass. And the press is gonna find some way to shaft
Nixon on this one.

PAT: It's not the press that matters. Nixon's wife is
proud of him.
He squeezes her hand.

HALDEMAN: And his staff. Come on, the copy they were
filing from China was great.

NIXON: Wait till the Mai-tais wear off.

EHRLICHMAN: The country's loving it.

NIXON: The hard-core four million 'Nixon nuts' aren't gonna go for it . . . They'll say I sold out to the Communists.

KISSINGER: You'll pick up the middle on this one – the Jews and Negroes.

NIXON: Jews and Negroes don't win elections, Henry. Better to hang them around the Democrats' necks.

HALDEMAN: The Jews aren't the middle, Henry. They're the far left.

NIXON: You're talking too much about black Africa, Henry. It's killing us with the rednecks.

HALDEMAN: The blacks are lost, the 'schwartzes' are gone . . .

NIXON: Don't let it lose us the right-wing vote . . .
A silence as the sour notes depress everyone.

NIXON (*feeling the deflation*): Hey, I sound like my father now. Let's have a drink!
Pat smiles. ZIEGLER *pokes his head in.*

ZIEGLER: Mr. President, the press guys asked if you could come back for a minute.

NIXON: The hell with 'em.

KISSINGER: I'll go back, Mr. President.
Everyone glares at Henry.

ZIEGLER: No, they want you, Mr. President. I really
    think it would be a good move.
    Nixon puts aside his drink, gets up.

NIXON: Gentlemen, I go now to discover the exact
    length, width, and depth of the shaft.

81. INT. AIR FORCE ONE. PRESS CABIN. SUNSET.
NIXON *closes the door behind him, turns.*
    DOZENS of REPORTERS stand, burst into applause.
*He is momentarily stunned, then he moves down the
aisle. Shaking hands. The reporters continue applauding.
Nixon, for once, is deeply moved. On the sound of
applause, we:*
    CUT TO:

82. EXT. JONES RANCH. TEXAS. DAY (1972).

REPORTER'S VOICE: J. Edgar Hoover is dead at the age of
    seventy-seven. The legendary crime buster served his
    country as Director of the FBI for almost half a
    century, from 1924 to 1972.
    *An enormous BRAHMA BULL, red-eyed, snorting,
    thrashes viciously against the reinforced walls of its
    pen.* NIXON *and* JACK JONES *watch as SECRET
    SERVICE hover nearby.*

JONES (V.O.): There's two kinds of bulls, Dick. Your
    good bull and your bad bull. This here's a bad bull.
    You piss him off, he'll kill everything in his path.

Only way to stop him is to shoot him.
*A WRANGLER climbs carefully into the chute. The
Brahma lunges for him.*

JONES: Eddie, you be damned careful with that beast.
His nuts are worth a helluva lot more'n yours.
He leads Nixon down the steps.

JONES (*cagey*): So, what's this about, Dick?

NIXON: It's me or Wallace, Jack. Wallace's third party is
only going to help McGovern. I need your support.

JONES: Well, you sure been chock full of surprises so far,
'Mister President.'

83. INT. JONES RANCH. LIVING ROOM. DAY (1972).
NIXON *and* HALDEMAN *are standing by the hearth. The
years have gone by but, in different clothing and
hairstyles, it is much the same group of a DOZEN
BUSINESSMEN gathered around, drinking Jack Daniels
and smoking cigars. Among them we recognize the*
CUBAN *and* MITCH. *It's heated.*

JONES: It looks like to me we're gonna lose a war for the
first Goddamn time and, Dick, Goddamnit, you're
going along with it, buying into this Kissinger
bullshit 'detente' with the Communists. 'Detente' – it
sounds like two fags dancing.

NIXON: Jack, we're not living in the same country you
and I knew in '46. Our people are just not gonna
sacrifice in major numbers for war. We can't even

148

get 'em to accept cuts in their gas tanks. Hell, the Arabs and the Japanese are bleeding the shit out of our gold . . .

JONES: And whose fault is that? If we'd won in Vietnam . . .

NIXON: It's nobody's fault, Jack. It's change – which is a fact of history. Even that old cocksucker Hoover's dead. Things change.
An uncomfortable silence. A servant brings coffee to Nixon, but Haldeman cuts him off. No one gets close to his guy.

MITCH: So . . . how's the food over there in China, Mr. Nixon?

NIXON: Free, if you're the president. *(nervous laughter)*

MITCH: What are you going to do about this Allende fellow nationalizing our businesses in Chile? You gonna send Kissinger down there?

NIXON: We're gonna get rid of him – Allende, I mean – just as fast as we can. He's on top of the list.

MITCH: How about Kissinger along with him?

NIXON: Kissinger's misunderstood. He pretends to be a liberal for his Establishment friends, but he's even tougher than I . . .

CUBAN: So Kissinger stays. Just like Castro, Mr. Nixon?

NIXON: Yeah, he stays . . .

*An uncomfortable silence. Jones walks closer to
Nixon.*

JONES: Desi's got a point. What the hell we gonna do
about the Communists right here in our backyard?!

NIXON: What do you mean, Jack?

JONES: I mean I got federal price controls on my oil. The
ragheads are beating the shit out of me. And I got
your EPA environment agency with its thumb so far
up my ass it's scratching my ear.

HALDEMAN: Gentlemen, I think it's about time for us to
be getting to the airport.

NIXON: Let him finish, Bob.

JONES: . . . And now I have a federal judge ordering me
to bus my kids halfway 'cross town to go to school
with some nigger kids. I think, Mr. President, you're
forgetting who put you where you are.

NIXON: The American people put me where I am.
Jones smirks. They all smirk. A dreadful moment.

JONES: Really? Well, that can be changed.
Dead silence. Nixon moves closer to Jones.

NIXON: Jack, I've learned that politics is the art of
compromise. I learned it the hard way. I don't know
if you have. But I tell you what, Jack . . . If you
don't like it, there's an election in November. You
can take your money out into the open, give it to
Wallace . . . How 'bout it Jack? Are you willing to

do that? Give this country over to some poet-pansy
socialist like George McGovern?
Nixon is right in Jones's face now.

NIXON: Because if you're uncomfortable with the EPA
up your ass, try the IRS . . .

JONES: Well, Goddamn. Are you threatening me, Dick?

NIXON (*softly*): Presidents don't threaten. They don't
have to. (*then*) Good day, gentlemen.
*As he walks out with Haldeman, there is a stone
silence.*

84. EXT. TEXAS LANDSCAPE. DAY.
*As the PRESIDENTIAL CAR pulls away in a three-car
entourage, we hear:*

REPORTERS (V.O.): . . . With George Wallace out of the
race, paralyzed by an assassin's bullet, Richard
Nixon has crushed George McGovern in the 1972
presidential election. It is the second biggest landslide
in American history, but . . .

85. EXT. AIR FORCE ONE. DAY (STOCK FOOTAGE).
The plane flying through clouds. A royal feeling.

REPORTERS (V.O.): . . . the Democrats have increased
their majority in the House and the Senate. As the
new term begins, there is mounting evidence of
strong hostility to President Nixon's mandate for a

'New American Revolution.' However, it does not seem that the Watergate investigations have, up to now, damaged Nixon politically in any significant way . . .

86. INT. AIR FORCE ONE. PRESIDENT'S CABIN. NIGHT.
NIXON *looks out the window, turns to* HALDEMAN *next to him, making notes on his ubiquitous clipboard.*
ZIEGLER *is nearby.*

NIXON: You know, they all miss the point. Probably our biggest achievement as an administration, when it's all said and done, isn't China or Russia. It's pulling out of Vietnam without a right-wing revolt.

HALDEMAN: I believe you're right, boss.

NIXON: . . . but even the presidency isn't enough anymore . . .

HALDEMAN: Sir?

NIXON: The presidency by itself won't protect us, Bob. We're beyond politics now . . .
Haldeman is puzzled. EHRLICHMAN *enters the cabin, excited, extending a cable. He is followed by long-haired* JOHN DEAN.

EHRLICHMAN: Sir, just in from Paris – the Vietnamese have accepted Henry's peace proposal. The bombing worked! They're caving.
Nixon reads Kissinger's cable, but he doesn't express any happiness.

HALDEMAN (*excited*): Congratulations, boss (*handshake offered*) – a great victory! The madman theory wasn't so crazy after all.

NIXON (*to himself*): This could be it . . . this could be it. Four long years . . .

EHRLICHMAN: Henry's on his way back to meet us. He wants to make sure he gets in all the photographs. Incidentally . . . maybe this isn't the right time but . . . uh, you should know . . . Bill Sullivan over at the FBI got back to us with his report on Kissinger.
Nixon looks up, interested.

EHRLICHMAN (*nods*): Yeah . . . Sullivan thinks Henry's leaking. He's the one

HALDEMAN: Yeah, I knew it. I knew it from '69 on, and I said it all along, didn't I . . .
Nixon's expression changes totally, narrowing, cold.

NIXON: No, you didn't, Bob . . .

EHRLICHMAN: Looks like he talked to Joe Kraft . . . and to the *Times*. Told them he was dead set against the bombing and that you were . . . 'unstable.' Claims he has to handle you 'with kid gloves' . . .
Waiting on Nixon, who goes into some inner state alone, dark brows furrowing with built-up rage.

HALDEMAN (*his darker side emerging*): So that explains his press notices. Working both sides of the fence: Jewboy Henry, always trying to get his Nobel Prize, get laid . . .

NIXON (*in his own world*): My God, my God! He talked
to the *New York Times*?

HALDEMAN: We ought to fire his whining ass. Right now
when he's on top. You know what – it'll set the right
example for the rest of this administration.

EHRLICHMAN: I would personally enjoy doing that, sir.

NIXON (*conflicted*): No, no. He's our only 'star' right
now. He'd go crying straight to the press. He'd
crucify us – the sonofabitch! . . . (*lethal*) Get
someone from on our staff on his ass. Tap his
phones. I want to know everyone he talks to.

HALDEMAN: Then we'll see how long the Kissinger
mystique lasts.
*In a foul mood now, paranoia setting in like a
storm cloud on his face, Nixon shifts back to
Dean, who is scared of this Nixon and tries to
pacify him.*

NIXON: So, what about those Watergate clowns, John?
This fucking Sirica's crazy. Thirty-five-year
sentences! There were no weapons. Right? No
injuries. There was no success! It's just ridiculous.

DEAN: Sirica's just trying to force one of them to testify.
But they're solid.

NIXON: Then what about this *Washington Post* crap?
Woodwind and Fernstein? (*Ziegler corrects him,
'Bernstein'*) Who the fuck are they? (*to Haldeman*)
Bob, are you working on revoking the *Post*'s

television license? *(Haldeman nods, 'Yes sir, I am.')* Good.

DEAN: Well, they're trying to connect Bob and John to a secret fund, but they don't have much.

HALDEMAN *(with a look to Ehrlichman)*: They don't have anything on us.

DEAN: The FBI's feeding me all their reports. I didn't think you should lose any more sleep on it, sir.

NIXON *(mutters, relieved)*: Good man, John, good man.
They all fall silent, feeling that false sense of security as the sound of the jet engines takes over. Suddenly, there is an air pocket and they rock back and forth.

87. INT. THE WHITE HOUSE. PRESS CONFERENCE. EAST ROOM. DAY.
SUBTITLE READS: 'JANUARY 1973.'
NIXON *is concluding his statement to the PRESS,* HALDEMAN *in the background with* ZIEGLER.

NIXON: . . . I can therefore announce that our long and tragic involvement in Vietnam is at an end. Our mission is accomplished, we have a cease-fire, our prisoners of war are coming back, and South Vietnam has the right to determine its own future. We have peace with honor.
The REPORTERS are immediately on their feet. A MONTAGE of QUICK CUTS follows to give the

impression of a hostile and never-ending barrage of
questions without satisfactory answers.

REPORTER 1 (*'Dan Rather'-type*): Sir, isn't it true little
has been achieved in this peace agreement that the
Communists have not been offering since 1969? That
in fact your administration has needlessly prolonged
the war and, at certain stages, has escalated it to new
levels of violence?
JUMP TO:

REPORTER 2 (*'Leslie Stahl'-type*): Mr. President, what is
your reaction to James McCord's statement that
high White House officials were involved in the
Watergate break-in?
JUMP TO:

REPORTER 3 (*'Sam Donaldson'-type*): Sir, the
Washington Post is reporting that Mr. Haldeman
and Mr. Ehrlichman have secretly disbursed up to
$900,000 in campaign funds. Is there any truth to
that?

NIXON (*snaps*): I've said before and I'll say again: I will
not respond to the charges of the *Washington Post*.
Nor will I comment on a matter that's currently
before the courts.

REPORTER 4: Do you intend to cooperate with Senator
Ervin's committee?

REPORTER 5: Will you agree to the appointment of a
special prosecutor?
The questions flood in. Nixon is overwhelmed. He

gathers his papers and starts to move off. A darkly funny thing happens: ZIEGLER *wanders into his path, almost colliding. Nixon, pissed, grabs Ziegler by the shoulders, spins him back towards the* REPORTERS, *and pushes him at them. Ziegler stumbles, looks confused.*

88. INT. OVAL OFFICE. THE WHITE HOUSE. DAY (1973).
NIXON *storms into his office, picking up an ashtray and hurling it across the room – it shatters against a wall. Everyone in the room with him –* KISSINGER, HALDEMAN, EHRLICHMAN *– is stunned.*

NIXON: I end the longest war in American history and they keep harping on this chickenshit! You know who's behind this, don't you – it's Teddy Kennedy! He drowns a broad in his car and he can't run for president.

EHRLICHMAN: He got pretty burned at Chappaquiddick.

NIXON: My point exactly! Somebody had to *die* before his shit got in the papers! Fucking Kennedys get away with everything. Do you see me screwing everything that moves? *(then)* For Christ's sake! I *did* what the *New York Times* editorial page said we should do! I ended the war, I got SALT I with the Russians, I opened China! So why are these cocksuckers turning on me? Because they don't like the way I look. Where I went to school.

HALDEMAN: Because they're not Americans.

NIXON: Right. They don't trust! They don't trust America!

HALDEMAN (*venting with him*): Why would they?! Who the hell's Sulzberger anyway? Their parents are gold traders from Eastern Europe. They buy things. They come to Jew York City and they buy up things. One of the things they buy is the *New York Times*. (*glares at Kissinger*) And you know what? Be proud because they'll never trust you, sir, because we speak for the average American.
Ehrlichman shares a look with Kissinger as Nixon and Haldeman feed into each other.

NIXON: You know why they're turning on me? They're not *serious* about power, that's why. They're playing with power. They're forgetting the national interest. In the old days, people knew how to hold power, how to set limits. They wouldn't have torn this country apart over a third-rate burglary. All they care about now are their egos, looking good at cocktail parties . . .

HALDEMAN: . . . beating out the other papers, chasing girls . . .

NIXON: . . . worrying whether someone said something 'nice' about them. All short-term, frivolous bullshit; Ben Bradlee worrying about Teddy Kennedy liking him . . .
Kissinger tries to get the focus back.

KISSINGER: Mr. President, I feel we're drifting toward

oblivion here. We're playing a totally reactive game; we've got to get ahead of the ball. *(pause, in an embarrassed voice)* We all know you're clean . . . Right? So let's do a housecleaning. Take the gloves off.

Haldeman shares a look with Ehrlichman. Is he referring to them? Nixon turns slowly on Kissinger, cryptic.

NIXON: Housecleaning? It would be ugly, Henry, really ugly . . .

KISSINGER: But it must be done; your government is paralyzed.

NIXON: All kinds of shit would come out. Like the Ellsberg thing. You knew about that Henry, didn't you?

KISSINGER *(vague)*: I . . . I heard something . . . It sounded idiotic.

NIXON: Idiotic? Yes, I suppose it was.

EHRLICHMAN: But you're the one who said we should expose him as some kind of sex fiend. Someone took you literally.

KISSINGER *(stung, and suddenly knowledgeable)*: I never suggested for some *imbeciles* to go break into a psychiatrist's office. How stupid of . . .

NIXON: That doesn't matter now, Henry. The point is, you might lose some of your media-darling halo if the press starts sniffing around our dirty laundry.

KISSINGER (*indignant*): I had nothing to do with that, sir, and I resent any implication . . .

NIXON: *Resent it* all you want, Henry, but you're in it with the rest of us. Cambodia, Ellsberg, the wiretaps you put in. The President wants you to know you can't just click your heels and head back to Harvard Yard. It's your *ass* too, Henry, and it's in the wind twisting with everyone else's.
A stony silence. The men, all clenched jaws, wait. Kissinger, icily, clicks his heels and withdraws.

KISSINGER (*at the door*): Mr. Nixon, it is possible for even a president to go too far.

NIXON: Yeah . . .
Nixon laughs maniacally. JOHN DEAN *crosses in as Kissinger exits. Dean closes the door behind him.*

HALDEMAN: You played it perfectly, sir – cocksucker! He's going to think twice before he leaks again.

NIXON (*exultant*): He'll be looking in his toilet bowl every time he pulls the chain.
They laugh madly, like hatters at a tea party.

DEAN (*worried*): Mr. President, Hunt wants more money. Another hundred-and-thirty thousand.

NIXON: Son of a bitch.

DEAN: He says if he doesn't get it right away, he's going to blow us out of the water. And he means it. Ever since his wife died in the plane crash, he's been over the edge.

NIXON: Pay him. Pay him what he wants.

HALDEMAN: We've got to turn the faucet off on this thing. It's out of control . . . *(as he crosses Dean, sotto voce)* You might burden just me with this in the future.

NIXON: It's Helms – it's got to be.

HALDEMAN: We could leverage Helms.

NIXON: How?

HALDEMAN: When I met with him, he said . . .

89. INT. CIA. HELMS'S OFFICE. DAY (FLASHBACK).
HELMS, *sitting across from* HALDEMAN.

HALDEMAN: . . this entire affair, the President wants you to know, is related to the Bay of Pigs, and if it opens up . . .
Helms grips the arms of his chair, leans forward excitedly, and yells at Haldeman.

HELMS: The Bay of Pigs had nothing to do with this! I have no concern about the Bay Of Pigs!!
Haldeman is shocked by Helms's violent reaction, but remains very cool.

HALDEMAN: This is what the President told me to relay to you, Mr. Helms.

HELMS *(settling back)*: All right . . .

161

90. INT. OVAL OFFICE. DAY (1973).
RESUME SCENE – HALDEMAN, EHRLICHMAN, DEAN, *and* NIXON.

HALDEMAN (*fishing*): . . . I was wondering what's such dynamite in this Bay of Pigs story? (*Nixon stares, nothing*) . . . although it was clearly effective, because all of a sudden it was no problem for Helms to go to the FBI and try to put a lid on Watergate.

NIXON: What about the documents he promised?

HALDEMAN: He'll give us the documents. (*then*) But I think he should be offered the ambassadorship to Iran. Then he'll go without a whimper.
Nixon stares at him, distracted.

NIXON: I promised Iran to Townsend.

HALDEMAN: Put Townsend in Belgium; it's available.

NIXON: Townsend gave us 300 grand. Belgium's not worth more than 100, 150 . . .

EHRLICHMAN: What about England?

NIXON: Forget it. Ehrenberg's paid three times that much . . .

HALDEMAN: Helms wants Iran or there might be problems. All his old CIA buddies are over there making a fortune off the Shah.

NIXON: For God's sake, when does this end?!

DEAN (*suddenly*): Executive clemency . . .

NIXON: What?

DEAN: Hunt has nothing to lose now. Pardon all of them. Nobody's going to investigate a crime for which the criminals have already been pardoned.

NIXON: I like that. That's a solution.

EHRLICHMAN: It'll never wash. Pardoning them means we're all guilty. The people, the press will go nuts.

NIXON: And what am I supposed to do? Just sit here and watch them coming closer? Eating their way to the center. (*paces*) Lyndon bugged! So did Kennedy! FDR cut a deal with Lucky Luciano. Christ, even Ike had a mistress! What's so special about me? (*then*) What about Lyndon? He could make a couple of calls to the Hill and shut this whole thing down. Did anyone talk to him?

HALDEMAN (*hesitant*): I did. He hit the roof. No dice. He says if you come out with the story about how he bugged your plane, he's going to reveal . . . (*he looks at Ehrlichman and Dean, pauses*)
We CUT ACROSS the room from Ehrlichman's point of view as Haldeman whispers the rest of the message in Nixon's ear.
Nixon's face goes ashen.

NIXON (*low key*): All right . . . all right.
He walks to the window.

NIXON (*to himself*): I don't know, I don't know . . . I just know we've made too many enemies.

EHRLICHMAN: Sir, Bob and I are gonna have to testify before Ervin's Committee.

NIXON: No, you're not! You're going to claim executive privilege and you're going to stonewall it all the way – plead the Fifth Amendment. I don't give a shit. They can't force the President's people to testify.

EHRLICHMAN: Executive privilege will make it look like we're covering up.

NIXON: We are covering up! For some petty, stupid shit. *(then)* There are things I can say – when other people say them, they'd be lies. But when I say them nobody believes me anyway . . .
Pause. A look between Haldeman and Ehrlichman, puzzled.

DEAN: Then we're going to have to give them Mitchell.
Nixon turns, stunned.

NIXON: Mitchell? Mitchell's . . . family.

DEAN: Either it goes to Mitchell or it comes here.
Nixon looks like he's been punched in the stomach.

HALDEMAN *(softly)*: John's right. It's not personal, boss. It's just the way the game is played. Sometimes you have to punt.
Nixon looks out the window. Suddenly, he looks very old and very tired in the gray Washington light.

NIXON: Jesus, I'm so Goddamn worn out with this . . .

91. INT. THE WHITE HOUSE. CORRIDOR. DAY.
HALDEMAN *and* EHRLICHMAN *leave the President's office. They're pensive, on the move. They come to a huddle next to a window in an isolated alcove.*

EHRLICHMAN: Who's gonna tell Mitchell?

HALDEMAN: You do it.

EHRLICHMAN: Why me?

HALDEMAN: 'Cause he hates you. It's worse when you get it from someone you trust.

EHRLICHMAN: He's wrong, you know – about Kennedy, LBJ, Truman.

HALDEMAN: How so?

EHRLICHMAN: Sure, they did stuff, but nothing like this, Bob. Forget Watergate, the break-ins, the Enemies List. You got an attempted firebombing at the Brookings Institution, planting McGovern stuff on the guy that shot Wallace, trying to slip LSD to Jack Anderson.

HALDEMAN: The 'Old Man' plays politics harder than anybody else.

EHRLICHMAN: You think this is just about politics?
They go inanimate as a White House STAFFER passes.

EHRLICHMAN (*privately*): You think LBJ would ever have asked Hunt to forge a cable implicating John Kennedy in the assassination of the President of

165

Vietnam? (*whispering fiercely*) How long have you know him, Bob? Twenty years? (*then*) You ever shake hands with him? You ever have a real conversation with him? We don't have a clue what's going on inside that man. And look what we're doing for him . . .

Ehrlichman glances around to make sure no one is listening. He leans close.

EHRLICHMAN: This is about Richard Nixon. You got people dying because he didn't make the varsity football team. You got the Constitution hanging by a thread because the 'Old Man' went to Whittier and not to Yale. (*then*) And what the hell is this 'Bay of Pigs' thing – he goes white every time it gets mentioned?

Haldeman, more bothered than he pretends, looks around.

HALDEMAN: It's a code or something.

EHRLICHMAN: I figured that out.

HALDEMAN (*low whisper*): I think he means the Kennedy assassination.

EHRLICHMAN: Yeah?

HALDEMAN: They went after Castro. In some crazy way it got turned on Kennedy. I don't think the 'P' knows what happened, but he's afraid to find out. It's got him shitting peach pits.

EHRLICHMAN: Christ, we created Frankenstein with those fucking Cubans.
Haldeman sighs, lets his guard down.

HALDEMAN: Eight words back in '72 – 'I covered up. I was wrong. I'm sorry' – and the American public would've forgiven him. But we never opened our mouths, John. We failed him.

EHRLICHMAN: Dick Nixon saying 'I'm sorry'? That'll be the day. The whole suit of armor'd fall off.

HALDEMAN: So you tell Mitchell . . .

92. EXT. WASHINGTON D.C. BRIDGE. NIGHT.
JOHN DEAN *stands at the center of the bridge, looks down at the Potomac.*

REPORTER (V.O.): Lyndon Johnson passed away today at 74 – one of the most tragic of American presidents . . .

HUNT (O.S.): You're early, John.
Dean jumps. Turns. HOWARD HUNT *is standing behind him.*

DEAN: I was sorry to hear about your wife.

HUNT (*a look*): Yes . . . I got the money.

DEAN: The President would like to know if that was the last payment.

HUNT: I'll bet he would.

DEAN: Is it?

HUNT (*a beat*): In Richard Nixon's long history of underhanded dealings, he has never gotten better value for his money. If I were to open my mouth, all the dominoes would fall.
Hunt starts to walk away.

DEAN: Can I ask you a question?
Hunt turns.

DEAN: How the hell do you have the temerity to blackmail the President of the United States?

HUNT: That's not the question, John. The question is: Why is he paying?

DEAN: To protect his people.

HUNT: I'm one of his people. The Cubans are his people. And we're going to jail for him.

DEAN: Howard, you'll serve no more than two years, then he'll pardon you.

HUNT (*lights his pipe*): John, sooner or later – sooner I think – you are going to learn the lesson that has been learned by everyone who has ever gotten close to Richard Nixon. That he's the darkness reaching out for the darkness. And eventually, it's either you or him. Look at the landscape of his life and you'll see a boneyard.
Hunt throws the match into the river.

HUNT: . . . And he's already digging your grave, John.

93. INT. THE WHITE HOUSE. CORRIDOR. DAY.
JOHN DEAN, *looking glum, walks down the corridors for his meeting with the President. Passing the SECRETARIES who look at him – that furtive look of people who sense crisis.*

REPORTERS (V.O.): FBI Director-designate, L. Patrick Gray, shocked the Senate by revealing that John Dean has been secretly receiving FBI reports on Watergate . . . Gray also said that Dean lied when he claimed Howard Hunt did not have an office in the White House . . .

94. INT. THE WHITE HOUSE. OVAL OFFICE. DAY.
SUBTITLE READS: 'MARCH 1973'
 DEAN *is explaining his new outlook to a quiet* NIXON.

DEAN: . . . this is the sort of thing Mafia people can do – washing money, and things like that. We just don't know about these things because we're not criminals. *On Nixon listening behind his desk, hands cupped over his mouth, frown across his face – the classic Nixon image of a deep thinker. The CAMERA drops to his desk. And moves towards a MIKE drilled in the edge of the desk.*
INTERCUT TO:

95. INT. FILE ROOM. BASEMENT. DAY.
A bank of TAPE RECORDERS labelled 'Oval Office,' 'Lincoln Room,' 'Phones 1-6,' 'EOB,' is rolling. BACK TO SCENE AT OPTION:

NIXON: How much do you need?

DEAN: Uh, I would say these people are going to cost a million dollars over the next two years . . .

NIXON: We could get that.

DEAN: Uh huh . . .

NIXON: We could get a million dollars. We could get it in cash. I know where it could be gotten.
INTERCUT: the TAPE rolling.

DEAN (*pause*): I'm still not confident we can ride through this. Some people are going to have to go to jail. Hunt's not the only problem. Haldeman let me use the $350,000 cash fund in his safe to make the payments. Ehrlichman had a role, a big role, in the Ellsberg break-in. And I'm . . . uh, I think it's time we begin to think in terms of cutting our losses.

NIXON (*worried about Dean*): You say, John, cut our losses and all the rest. But suppose the thing blows and they indict Bob and the others. Jesus, you'd never recover from that, John. It's better to fight it out instead, and not let people testify . . .

DEAN: Sir, I still don't think, uh, we can contain it anymore. There's a cancer on the presidency. And it's growing. With every day that . . .

NIXON: Jesus, everything is a crisis among the upper intellectual types, the softheads. The average people don't think it's much of a crisis. For Christ's sake it's

not Vietnam . . . no one's dying here. Isn't it
ridiculous?

DEAN: I agree it's ridiculous but –

NIXON: I mean, who the hell cares about this penny-ante
shit. Goldwater put it right. He said: 'Well for
Christ's sakes, everybody bugs everybody else; we
know that.' . . . It's the cover-up, not the deed that's
really bad here. *(then)* If only Mitchell could step up
and take the brunt of it; give them the hors d'oeuvre
and maybe they won't come back for the main
course. That's the tragedy in all this. Mitchell's
going to get it in the neck anyway. It's time he
assumed responsibility.
Dean has a nervous look in his eye.

DEAN: He won't. He told Ehrlichman he won't.
A lightning-like IMAGE reveals MITCHELL,
responding to EHRLICHMAN. *This is Nixon's mind at
work.*

MITCHELL: You tell Brother Dick I got suckered into this
thing by not paying attention to what these bastards
were doing. I don't have a guilty conscience . . . And
he shouldn't either.
*Nixon glances towards the microphone as he moves
around the desk to get closer to Dean.*

NIXON *(loud and clear)*: He's right. Maybe it's time to
go the hang-out route, John. A full and thorough
investigation . . . We've cooperated with the FBI,

we'll cooperate with the Senate. What do we have to hide?

DEAN (*prompted*): No, we have nothing to hide.

NIXON (*repeating*): We have nothing to hide. *(then)* But the only flaw in the plan is that they're not going to believe the truth. That is the incredible thing!
Dean, who is worried about his own hide if the truth comes out, sees the point of this.

DEAN: I agree. It's tricky. Everything seems to lead back here, and, uh . . . people would never understand.
Nixon awkwardly puts his arm around Dean's shoulder. Dean begins to sense a betrayal in the offing.

NIXON: John, I want you to get away from this madhouse, these reporters, and go up to Camp David for the weekend. And I want you to write up a report. I want you to put everything you know about Watergate in there. Say: Mr. President, here it all is.
Another lightning-like IMAGE is Nixon's worst fear – JOHN DEAN is at a table, plea-bargaining with TWO PROSECUTORS, their backs to us.

DEAN (*V.O.*): You want me to put it all in writing? Over my signature?

NIXON (*V.O.*): Nobody knows more about this thing than you do, John.
A pause.

DEAN: I'm not going to be the scapegoat for this. Haldeman and Ehrlichman are in it just as deep as me.

NIXON: John, you don't want to start down that road. I remember what Whittaker Chambers told me back in '48 – and he was a man who suffered greatly – he said, 'On the road of the informer, it's always night.' *(then)* This is beyond you or even me. It's the country, John. It's the presidency.

DEAN: I understand that, sir.

NIXON: Good. You know how I feel about loyalty. I'm not going to let any of my people go to jail. That I promise you. *(moves closer)* The important thing is to keep this away from Haldeman and Ehrlichman. I'm trusting you to do that, John. I have complete confidence in you.
Off Dean's face we:
CUT TO:

96. TELEVISION SCREEN. NIXON. NIGHT (1973).
NIXON *on the TV screen, shaken, ashen-faced.*

NIXON: I was determined that we should get to the bottom of Watergate, and the truth should be fully brought out no matter who was involved . . .

97. INT. CIA. HELMS'S OFFICE. NIGHT (1973).
RICHARD HELMS, *absently watching* NIXON *on TV,*

carries a handful of documents to a CIA incinerator. He drops them in the fire, watches them burn.

NIXON (*on TV, struggles*): Today, in one of the most difficult decisions of my presidency, I accepted the resignations of two of my closest associates – Bob Haldeman and John Ehrlichman – two of the finest public servants it has been my privilege to know . . . The counsel to the President, John Dean, has also resigned.
CLOSE on Helms burning documents.

98.
LIMBO – HALDEMAN *watches TV, his* WIFE *and* CHILDREN *next to him. He thinks back to:*

INT. EXEC. OFFICE BLDG. NIXON OFFICE. NIGHT
(FLASHBACK).

Haldeman's mind – the last one-on-one session.
HALDEMAN *leaves the office, looking back over his shoulder at* NIXON *alone in the gathering shad*ows.

HALDEMAN: More light, chief?

NIXON (*distracted, waves*): No . . .
Haldeman exits.
BACK TO SCENE.

NIXON (*V.O.*): . . . There can be no whitewash at the White House . . . two wrongs do not make a right. I love America. God bless America and God bless each and every one of you.

HALDEMAN (*to himself*): Six . . . six bodies.
His wife puts her hand on his knee in support. He squeezes her hand.

99.
LIMBO – EHRLICHMAN *also watches, with* FAMILY.

100. INT. THE WHITE HOUSE. OVAL OFFICE. NIGHT.
NIXON *sits at his desk, holding a rigid expression.*

FLOOR MANAGER (O.S.): And . . . we're clear.
We stay on Nixon as the film lights go off, leaving him in shadow. He is devastated.
ALEXANDER HAIG, *Nixon's new chief-of-staff, seen earlier, watches Nixon for a moment, turns to the* VIDEO CREW.

HAIG (*softly*): Out.

101. INT. THE WHITE HOUSE. DINING-ROOM. NIGHT (1973).
NIXON *at one end of the lengthy table,* PAT *at the other eat, in a dreadful silence, attended by* MANOLO *and* SERVANTS *who move nervously, anxious to have the dinner over with.*

PAT (*at last*): I'm giving a tea for the wives of the POWs.
Nixon doesn't respond.

PAT: Are you going to Key Biscayne?
Nixon doesn't look up.

NIXON: Yes.

PAT: When?

NIXON: Tomorrow.

PAT: Ron told me that Bob Haldeman's been calling. But you won't talk to him . . . If he's convicted, will you pardon him?

NIXON: No.
She looks at him.

PAT: . . . Why are you cutting yourself off from the rest of us? *(then)* Can't we discuss this?
Nixon slowly sets his spoon down. An icy stare.

NIXON: What exactly did you want to discuss, Pat?

PAT: You. What you're doing –

NIXON *(interrupts)*: And what *am* I doing?

PAT: I wish I knew. You're hiding.

NIXON: Hiding what?

PAT: Whatever it is you've always been hiding. You're letting it destroy you, Dick. You won't even ask for help. You're destroying *yourself*, Dick.
Nixon pauses, rings the dinner bell. Manolo reappears at the door.

NIXON: Mrs. Nixon is finished.

Pat looks as if she's been slapped; slowly puts down her silverware. Manolo clears away her plate.

PAT: I'm the only one left, Dick. If you don't talk to me, you . . .

NIXON: Brezhnev's coming in three days. I don't want to deal with *them*. And *him*. And *you*.
Pat sits rigid for a moment.

PAT: How much more? How much more is it going to cost? When do the rest of us stop paying off your debts?
Nixon puts down his fork, embarrassed. Manolo has beaten a hasty retreat.

NIXON: I'd like to finish my dinner in peace. It's not too much to ask.
Pat stands slowly.

PAT: No, it isn't. I won't interfere with you anymore. I'm finished trying.

NIXON: Thank you.

PAT (*incredulous*): Thank you? (*then*) Dick, sometimes I understand why they hate you.
Nixon watches her walk out the door. Then, he picks up his fork and continues eating.

SENATOR SAM ERVIN (*V.O.: drawls*): the Senate Select Committee on Watergate will come to order . . .
A gavel POUNDS O.S.

177

102. INT. THE WHITE HOUSE. HAIG'S OFFICE. DAY.
*NIXON STAFFERS are gathered around Haig's TV set
as we:*
   CROSSCUT TO:

103. INT. COMMITTEE CHAMBER. (SEEN ONLY ON TV).
DAY (1973).
JOHN DEAN *reads his statement to the* COMMITTEE.
*Conservatively groomed, horn-rimmed glasses, shorter
hair, Dean speaks in a monotone. A pretty blond
woman, his WIFE, sits noticeably behind him.*

DEAN (*on TV*): . . . it was a tremendous disappointment
   to me because it was quite clear that the cover-up, as
   far as the White House was concerned, was going to
   continue . . .

STAFFERS: Lying sack of shit! Little mommy's boy – go
   tell the teacher, will ya . . .
   HAIG *looks at Dean on TV, shakes his head,
   disgusted, and goes out.*

HAIG: The weasel's got no proof. Just remember that it's
   still an informer's word against the President's.

104. INT. THE WHITE HOUSE. CORRIDOR. DAY.
HAIG *walking past STAFF into the Oval Office:*

DEAN (*droning on, V.O./TV*): . . . it was apparent to me
   I had failed in turning the President around . . . I
   reached the conclusion that Ehrlichman would never

admit to his involvement in the cover-up . . . I
assumed that Haldeman would not, because he
would believe it a higher duty to protect the
President . . .

105. INT. THE WHITE HOUSE. OVAL OFFICE. DAY (1973).
HAIG *slides into the room where* NIXON *and* LEONID
BREZHNEV, *Premier of the USSR, are engaged in a
friendly meeting through an INTERPRETER.* ANDREI
GROMYKO *completes the glum Soviet threesome.*

BREZHNEV (*in Russian*): . . . Mao told me in 1963: 'If I
have nuclear weapons, let 400 million Chinese die,
300 million will be left.' *(leans closer)* Mao suffers
from a mental disorder; we know this a long time in
my country. *(then)* This is the man you want to be
your ally?

NIXON: He was *your* ally for twenty years, Leonid.

BREZHNEV (*makes a funny gesture*): Yes, yes, Dick. Life
is always the best teacher, you know this and you
too will discover how treacherous he can be. But it
must not interfere with the building of a SALT II
treaty between our great countries. Peace in our era
is possible . . .
*Nixon looks to Haig, who whispers something in his
ear.*

NIXON: Excuse me, Mr. Chairman.
*Nixon and Haig move to a corner of the room,
whisper.*

BREZHNEV (*to Gromyko*): If Haldeman and Ehrlichman are indicted, it will wound him, perhaps fatally.

GROMYKO: That depends on who they believe – Nixon or Dean.
Brezhnev looks at Nixon, who is visibly shaken.

BREZHNEV (*shakes his head*): Incredible. He looks like a man with little time left.

106. INT. THE WHITE HOUSE. NIXON BEDROOM. NIGHT (1973).
Nixon's daughter, JULIE, *earnest, bright-eyed, looks at her Father.*

JULIE (*hesitantly*): Did you . . . Daddy? Did you cover it up?
NIXON *looks at her steadily.*

NIXON: Do you think I would do something like that, honey?
Julie shakes her head vigorously, then puts her hands to her eyes.

JULIE: Then you can't resign! You just can't. You're one of the best presidents this country's ever had! You've done what Lincoln did. You've brought this country back from civil war! You can't let your enemies tear you down! (*calmer*) You've got to stay and fight. I'll go out there and make speeches, Dad. No one knows the real you. How sweet you are, how nice you are to people. I'll tell them.

She embraces him almost desperately, kissing him on the forehead, crying.

JULIE: Daddy, you are the most decent person I know.

NIXON (*over her shoulder*): I hope I haven't let you down.

JULIE (*hugging him through her tears*): They just don't know; they don't know the real you.
On Nixon – CLOSE.

107. INT. THE WHITE HOUSE. PAT'S BEDROOM. DAY (1973).
PAT is still wearing her nightdress, coffee and cigarette in hand, as her press secretary, HELEN SMITH, runs through a sheaf of papers. A TELEVISION drones in the background.

SMITH (*cheery*): . . . and on Friday we have the high-school students from Ohio, Saturday is the Women's National Republican Club . . .

NEWSCASTER I (*V.O.*): In a development that could break Watergate wide open, former White House aide, Alexander Butterfield, testifying today before the Senate Select Committee, revealed the existence of a taping system that may have recorded conversations in the White House, the EOB, and the Camp David retreat . . .
Pat glances up over the top of her glasses.

SMITH (*continues*): And on Sunday you're saying hello to
the VFW Poppy Girl . . .
She realizes Pat is not listening.

SMITH: Mrs. Nixon . . .?
*CLOSE: on Pat as she slowly raises a hand to her
lips.*

NEWSCASTER 1 (*V.O.*): White House sources say that for
the past three years, President Nixon has recorded
virtually every conversation he has had, including
those with his staff, and even members of his own
family . . .
Pat is horrified.

108. INT. THE WHITE HOUSE. PRESIDENT'S BEDROOM.
DAY.
NIXON *sits in his bed, alone, still in his pajamas. It's
clear he hasn't slept. He looks shell-shocked.*

NEWSCASTER 1 (*V.O.*): This is a stunning revelation. If
such tapes exist, they could tell us once and for all:
What did the President know and when did he know
it . . .
The CAMERA closing on NIXON. *His deepest secrets
are now being revealed. He begins coughing
violently. He tries to cover his mouth, but notices
now that his hand and the sheets around him are
covered with blood. He screams, terrified.*

NIXON: Oh God – Pat!
HARD CUT TO:

109. INT. BETHESDA NAVAL HOSPITAL CORRIDOR. DAY (1973).

NIXON *on a gurney, being wheeled down a hospital corridor.* PAT, *wearing dark sunglasses, is with him, very concerned. A plastic mask is over his face.*

He struggles to get up, but a NURSE gently presses him back down. SECRET SERVICE AGENTS surround the gurney. HAIG *clears the corridors nervously.*

HAIG: Clear the path! The President is coming through. Clear a path. I'm in charge here.

Pat gets the DOCTOR's *attention on the move.*

PAT (*privately*): Is it TB?

DOCTOR: No.

PAT: He's sure he has tuberculosis.

DOCTOR: No, it's an acute viral pneumonia (*lowers his voice*). But that's not what we're worried about. We found an inflammation in his left leg. It's phlebitis . . .

CLOSE on Nixon, eyes closed, the overhead lights reflect in the mask.

REPORTERS (V.O.): Watergate Special Prosecutor Archibald Cox has broadened his investigation to include President Nixon's business dealings and house payments. Nixon apparently paid no income tax in the years 1970, '71, and '72 . . . and may have illegally used government funds to improve his San Clemente Western White House.

Haig holds open the doors as the ORDERLIES push Nixon into the respiratory unit.

110. INT. BETHESDA NAVAL HOSPITAL. RESPIRATORY
UNIT. DAY.

A DOCTOR *and* NURSE *remove the mask from*
NIXON's *face.*

REPORTERS (V.O.): Attorney General Elliot Richardson
     will present evidence to a grand jury that Vice
     President Agnew is guilty of bribery, extortion and
     tax evasion . . .
     *Nixon immediately starts gasping. He again tries to
     rise, but hands push him back. The doctor fits the
     mouthpiece of a respirator into Nixon's mouth.
     Images of the Beast pervade the room.
     Nixon begins breathing . . . His eyes going past* PAT
     to . . .
     IMAGES OF THE PAST – OF HIS PARENTS,
     FRANK, HANNAH, LITTLE ARTHUR, HAROLD
     . . . THE GROCERY STORE.
     INTERCUT WITH:

111. EXT. STREET. DAY.
MARTHA MITCHELL *is acting strangely behind enormous
sunglasses – at an impromptu interview on the* STREET.

MARTHA: . . . Can you keep a secret, honey? 'Tween
     you, me, and the gatepost, Tricky Dick *always* knew
     what was going on . . . every last Goddamn detail.
     And my husband's not taking the rap this time . . .
     They know they can't shut me up, so they'll
     probably end up killing me, but I depend on you, the

press, to protect me . . . and my husband, because
that's what it's going to come to . . .
INTERCUT WITH:

112. EXT. STREET. DAY.
JOHN MITCHELL, *angry, beleaguered, bypasses cameras
outside a COURTHOUSE.*

MITCHELL: She doesn't know what she's talking about.
Stop bothering her. She's not well. Hell, she's nuts —
you bastards've seen to that. *(brushing past another
question)* You can stick it right back up your keester
fella. Our marriage is finished, thank you very much
. . . *(pushes on)*
BACK TO:

113.
NIXON in the hospital, breathing.

REPORTER *(V.O.)*: Archibald Cox declared war on
President Nixon today by issuing a subpoena for
nine of the President's tapes . . .

NIXON *(V.O., yells)*: Never! Over my dead body!

114. INT. THE WHITE HOUSE. WEST WING CORRIDOR. DAY
(1973).
NIXON, *his leg swollen, limps down the corridor,
furious.* HAIG *walks with him,* ZIEGLER *and the lawyer,*

BUZHARDT, *bringing up the rear. Haig clears the corridor of potential eavesdroppers.*

NIXON: It's the President's personal property! I will never give up my tapes to a bunch of Kennedy-loving Harvard Democrat cocksuckers!

HAIG: This could trigger the impeachment. They'll go to the Supreme Court next.

NIXON: Let 'em try! I appointed three of those bastards! I'm not giving 'em my tapes!

HAIG: Can the president afford to ignore a subpoena?

NIXON: Who the fuck does Cox think he is? *(fumes)* I never made a dime from public office! I'm honest. My dad died broke. You know the sonofabitch went to law school with Jack Kennedy? . . . The last gasp of the Establishment! They got the hell kicked out of 'em in the election, so now they gotta squeal about Watergate cause we were the first real threat to them in years. And by God, Al, we would have changed it, changed it so they couldn't have changed it back in a hundred years, if only . . .

HAIG: Congress is considering four articles of impeachment, sir.

NIXON: For what?!

BUZHARDT: Sir, the charges are serious – first, abuse of power; second, obstruction of justice; third, failure to cooperate with Congress; and last, bombing Cambodia . . .

NIXON: They can't impeach me for bombing Cambodia. The President can bomb anybody he wants.

ZIEGLER: That's true . . .

BUZHARDT: Sir, we'll win that one, but the other three . . .

NIXON: You know, Fred, they sell tickets.

ZIEGLER: Sir?

NIXON: They sell tickets to an impeachment. Like a fucking circus . . . Okay, so they impeach me. Then it's a question of mathematics. How many votes do we have in the Senate?
A beat. Then:

HAIG: About a dozen.

NIXON (*wounded*): A dozen? I got half of 'em elected. I still got the South and Goldwater and his boys. I'll take my chances in the Senate.

ZIEGLER: We should . . .

HAIG: Then we'll have to deal with the possibility of removal from office, loss of pension, possibly . . . prison.

NIXON: Shit, plenty of people did their best writing in prison. Gandhi, Lenin . . .

ZIEGLER: That's right.

NIXON (*beat, glowers darkly*): What I know about this country, I . . . I could rip it apart. If they want a public humiliation, that's what they'll get. But I will

never resign this office. Where the fuck am I?
They look at him strangely. They've stopped at the
doors of the East Room. The SOUND of VOICES
and a VIOLIN playing inside.

NIXON (*to Ziegler*): What's in there?

ZIEGLER: POWs. And their families.

NIXON: So I'm supposed to be . . .

ZIEGLER: Compassionate. Grateful.

NIXON: Proud?

ZIEGLER (*confused*): Sir?

NIXON: Of them.

ZIEGLER: Yes, yes.

NIXON (*back to Haig, bitterly*): Fire him.

HAIG: Who?

NIXON: Cox! Fire him.

HAIG: But he works for the Attorney General. Only
Richardson can fire him.

BUZHARDT (*concerned*): Sir, if I may . . . echo my
concern . . .

NIXON (*ignoring Buzhardt, to Haig*): Then tell
Richardson to fire him.

HAIG: Richardson won't do that. He'll resign.

NIXON: The hell he will! Fire him too. If you have to go

all the way down to the janitor at the Justice
Department, fire the sonofabitch! And . . .

ZIEGLER: He's asked for it.

HAIG: May I just say something, sir? I think you should
welcome the subpoena. The tapes can only prove
that Dean is a liar.

ZIEGLER: That's right, sir.
A moment.

NIXON: There's more . . . there's more than just me. You
can't break, my boy, even when there's nothing left.
You can't admit, even to yourself, that it's gone, Al.
(pointing to the East Room) Do you think those
POWs in there did?

ZIEGLER: No, sir . . .

NIXON: Now some people, we both know them, Al,
think you can go stand in the middle of the bullring
and cry, 'Mea culpa, mea culpa,' while the crowd is
hissing and booing and spitting on you. But a man
doesn't cry. *(then)* I don't cry. You don't cry . . .
You fight!
*INTERCUT soft IMAGES over NIXON being
pounded at FOOTBALL . . .*
*Nixon straightens himself, puts on a smile, nods to
Ziegler. Ziegler opens the door. A ROAR of
CHEERS and MARTIAL MUSIC greets the
President, as he disappears inside.*

189

TV SCREEN. NBC LOGO. LIMBO.

ANNOUNCER (*V.O.*): We interrupt this program for a special report from NBC News.
A REPORTER appears, stunned.

REPORTER (*V.O.*): The country tonight is in the midst of what may be the most serious constitutional crisis in history. In the wake of Vice President Spiro Agnew's forced resignation on charges of corruption, President Nixon has fired Special Prosecutor Archibald Cox.
DOCUMENTARY IMAGES. ARCHIBALD COX walking in the street, having heard the news, smiling.

REPORTER (*V.O., contd*): Attorney General Elliot Richardson has resigned rather than comply with the President's order, and Deputy Attorney General William Ruckelshaus was fired when he refused to carry out the order . . .
DOCUMENTARY IMAGES – FBI AGENTS carrying boxes of files out of the Special Prosecutor's office. RUCKELSHAUS getting into a car, refusing to comment. ELLIOT RICHARDSON moving down a gauntlet of REPORTERS. We CUT BACK to the REPORTER on camera, grim.

REPORTER (*on TV, cont'd*): Tonight, the country, without a Vice President, stands poised at a crossroads – has a government of laws become a government of one man?

116. EXT. THE WHITE HOUSE. NIGHT. 1973.
*As before, the black iron bars. The facade of the
mansion. The light in the second floor. We move in
slowly.*

117. INT. THE WHITE HOUSE. LINCOLN SITTING ROOM.
NIGHT (1973).
NIXON *is really drunk now, listening to some
GIBBERISH on the tape. We move in on his profile,
framed by Lincoln in the background We should not be
able to make out the voices — occasional words like
'Castro,' 'Kennedy.' But that's about it . . . nothing
more. And as we move closer on Nixon, bleary-eyed,
we should feel he has no idea, either, of what he's
listening to. It's just . . . noise. PAT's voice cuts in. She's
standing at the doorway. She's been drinking too, but is
sharp.*

PAT: They're like love letters. You should burn them.
*Nixon, startled, tries to shut off the tape, but he hits
the wrong button and we hear high-speed VOICES
in reverse.*

PAT: Why didn't you?

NIXON (*slurs*): You can't expect me to explain that to
you.

PAT: What matters to me is whether you understand it.
A beat. He finally gets the tape stopped.

191

NIXON: They're evidence. You can't legally destroy evidence.
Pat stares at him.

PAT: You don't expect me to believe that for one minute, do you? *(then)* Does it matter what's on them? Really? . . . Murder, Dick? Sex? Your secrets, your fantasies? Or just me and you and . . .

NIXON: Don't be ridiculous!

PAT: I remember Alger Hiss. I know how ugly you can be – you're capable of anything. But you see, it doesn't really matter, at the end of the day, what's on them. Because you have absolutely no remorse. No concept of remorse. You want the tapes to get out, you want them to see you at your worst . . .

NIXON: You're drunk! *(Pat laughs, 'Yeah, I am.')* No one will ever see those tapes. Including you!
A beat.

PAT: And what would I find out that I haven't known for years. *(then)* What makes it so damn sad is that you couldn't confide in any of us. You had to make a record . . . for the whole world.

NIXON: They were for me. They're mine.

PAT: No. They're not *yours*. They *are* you. You should burn them.
She turns and walks out. Nixon is turbulent, upset. He turns and suddenly sees the ghost of his young

mother, HANNAH, *sitting there in the shadows,*
staring at him.
He jumps. Those eyes of hers. Penetrating, gazing
right through him.

HANNAH: What has changed in thee, Richard . . . When
thou were a boy . . .

NIXON (*blurts out*): No! Please! Don't talk to me!
Anything . . . but *don't talk to me.*
A SHARP CUT snaps us from this reverie, and
Nixon is alone in his sitting room, the door closed,
the VOICE on the tape droning. He downs pills with
the Scotch.

NIXON (*V.O. on tape*): . . . these guys went after Castro.
Seven times, ten times . . . What do you think –
people like that, they just give up? They just walk
away? (*then*) Whoever killed Kennedy came from
this . . . this *thing* we created. This Beast . . . That's
why we can't let this thing go any farther . . .
He looks over at the recorder, slowly turning. He
pushes 'Stop' and then runs it back on 'Rewind.'
High-speed voices. He pushes 'Stop' again. A series
of TIME CUTS shows Nixon getting drunker.
Playing sections of the tape. The camera closes on
the tape machine. It's all a blur as we hear a HUM
growing louder and louder, as we inch in on an
abstract CLOSE-UP of the TAPE moving across the
capstan.

REPORTER (*V.O.*): In the latest bombshell, the President's

lawyers revealed that there is an eighteen-and-a-half-minute gap in a critical Watergate tape . . .

118. INT. THE WHITE HOUSE. WEST WING. DAY (1974).
A frenzy of paperwork as the PRESIDENT'S LAWYERS – BUZHARDT and ST. CLAIR – sit hunched around a table piled with transcripts, helped by TWO YOUNG ASSISTANTS.

NIXON *is aghast as he reads some of the highlighted sections.* HAIG *and* ZIEGLER *attend.*

REPORTER 1 (V.O.): . . . In an attempt to head off impeachment proceedings, the President has agreed to release transcripts of forty-six taped conversations . . .

REPORTER 2 (V.O.): . . . In a simple ceremony, Gerald Ford was sworn in as Vice President. A longtime, popular member of Congress, Ford reinforces a sense of . . .

REPORTER 3 (V.O.): . . . citing White House wrongdoing, the judge has dismissed all charges against Daniel Ellsberg.

REPORTER 4 (V.O.): . . . the grand jury has indicted former Nixon aides Bob Haldeman, John Ehrlichman, and former Attorney General John Mitchell . . .
Nixon shakes the paper in the faces of Buzhardt and St. Clair.

NIXON: You're lawyers. How can you let this shit go by! *(points)* Look! This? Nixon can't say this.

BUZHARDT: You did say it, sir.

NIXON: Never. I never said that about Jews!
Buzhardt glances at St. Clair.

BUZHARDT: We could check the tape again, sir.

NIXON: You don't need to check the tape. I know what I said.
He grabs the Magic Marker out of the lawyer's hand and furiously blacks out an entire section.

NIXON: And this?! Good Lord, have you lost your mind? Nixon can't say this. 'Niggers'!

ZIEGLER: Well, we could delete it.

ST. CLAIR: We're doing the best we can, sir.

NIXON: Well it's not good enough . . .

ST. CLAIR: We can black it out.

ZIEGLER: Or we could write 'expletive deleted.'

NIXON: . . . and get rid of all these 'Goddamns' and 'Jesus Christs'!

ST. CLAIR: Sir, all these deletion marks in the transcripts will make it look like you swear all the time.
Nixon grows cold, stares steadily at St. Clair.

NIXON: For Christ's sake, it soils my mother's memory. Do you think I want the whole Goddamn world to see my mother like this? Raising a dirty mouth!

BUZHARDT: But sir, we'll have to start over from the beginning. We don't have the staff to . . .
Nixon loses it, sweeps the piles of transcripts off the table. They fly around the office.

NIXON (*screams*): Then start over! The world will see only what I show them. From page one!

119. INT. THE WHITE HOUSE. OVAL OFFICE. NIGHT (1974).
NIXON *sits at his desk, grimacing tightly into the TV CAMERA. Next to him is a stack of blue binders emblazoned with the presidential seal.*

NIXON: Good evening, my fellow Americans. Tonight I'm taking an action unprecedented in the history of this office . . .

120. INT. THE WHITE HOUSE. HAIG'S OFFICE. NIGHT (1974).
KISSINGER *and* HAIG *watch* NIXON *on television. They share a drink.*

NIXON (*on TV, continues*): . . . an action that will at last, once and for all, show that what I knew and what I did with regard to the Watergate break-in and cover-up were just as I have described them to you from the very beginning . . .

HAIG: He's completely lost touch with reality.

NIXON (*on TV, cont'd*): . . . I had no knowledge of the cover-up until John Dean told me about it on March twenty-first. And I did not intend that payment to Hunt or anyone else be made . . .

KISSINGER: Can you imagine what this man would have been had he ever been loved?

NIXON (*on TV, cont'd*): . . . because people have got to know whether or not their President is a crook. Well, I am not a crook. I have never made a dime from public service . . .

KISSINGER: Oh God, I'm going to throw up.

HAIG: They'll crucify him . . .
    Kissinger turns to Haig.

KISSINGER: Does anybody care anymore? (*then*) What happens after . . .?
    They share a look.
    INTERCUT TO:

121. INT. THE WHITE HOUSE. PAT'S BEDROOM. NIGHT.
PAT *sits alone, drinking, as the television drones on with the latest invasion of her privacy. As we move in, we see the spirit drawn out of her. She seems numb.*

122. DOCUMENTARY IMAGE. EXT. THE WHITE HOUSE.
NIGHT (1974).

REPORTERS (V.O.): The Supreme Court ruled today
eight-to-zero that President Nixon's claims of
'executive privilege' cannot be used in criminal cases,
and that he must turn over all subpoenaed tapes . . .
a firestorm on Capitol Hill as . . .

123. INT. THE WHITE HOUSE. CORRIDORS & STAIRS.
NIGHT (1974).
*SUBTITLE READS: 'JULY 1974,' over EMPTY SHOTS
of an EMPTY HOUSE, filled with gloom and dread. The
FOOTSTEPS of two silhouettes crack the silence as they
make their way towards the Lincoln Sitting Room. It is
an eerie echo of the film's opening shots of the White
House. The silhouettes now become apparent as*
GENERAL HAIG *and* HENRY KISSINGER.

REPORTERS (V.O.): . . . The House Judiciary Committee
has voted twenty-seven-to-eleven to recommend
impeachment to the full House. The deliberations
now go to the House floor . . . In its report, the
Committee offers evidence that Nixon obstructed
justice on at least thirty-six occasions, that he
encouraged his aides to commit perjury, and that he
abused the powers of his office . . . In a separate
report, the Senate Select Committee details the
misuse of the IRS, the FBI, the CIA and the Justice

Department. It denounces the Plumbers, and it raises the question of whether the United States had a valid election in 1972.

HIGH ANGLE – Haig knocks and enters the Lincoln Sitting Room. A shaft of LIGHT from inside zigzags the darkness. And we hear a snatch of LOUD MUSIC before the door is closed.

124. INT. THE WHITE HOUSE. LINCOLN SITTING ROOM. NIGHT (1974).

NIXON sits in his chair in a suit and tie, listening to 'Victory at Sea' at top volume. In front of him is a picture album – 1922 portraits of the NIXON FAMILY – HAROLD holding ARTHUR. RICHARD stares glumly at the camera between HANNAH and FRANK.

GENERAL HAIG, *with* KISSINGER *behind, approaches with some papers held out in his hand. Nixon sees them, turns down the hi-fi.*

NIXON: 'Victory At Sea,' Al . . . Henry. The Pacific Theater. Christ, you can almost feel the waves breaking over the decks.

HAIG: I'm afraid we have another problem, Mr. President.
He hands him a paper. Nixon glances at it.

HAIG: June twenty-third, '72, sir. The part that's underlined. Your instructions to Haldeman regarding the CIA and the FBI.

NIXON: So?

HAIG: Your lawyers feel it's the . . . 'smoking gun.'

NIXON: It's totally out of context. I was protecting the national security, I never intended –

HAIG: Sir, the deadline is today.

NIXON: Can we get around this, Al?

HAIG: It's the Supreme Court, sir; you don't get around it.
Nixon, silenced, looks down at the paper in his hands and sighs.

HAIG: If you resign, you can keep your tapes as a private citizen . . . You can fight them for years.

NIXON: And if I stay?
A long moment.

HAIG: You have the army.
Nixon looks up at him, then over at Henry.

NIXON: The army?

HAIG: Lincoln used it.

NIXON: That was civil war.

HAIG: How do you see this?
Nixon closes his eyes. Haig takes the transcript back.

HAIG: We can't survive this, sir. They also have you instructing Dean to make the payoff to Hunt.

NIXON: There is nothing in that statement the President can't explain.

HAIG: Sir, you talked about opening up the whole 'Bay of Pigs' thing again.

NIXON: That's right . . .

HAIG: Three days before, on the June twentieth tape – the one with the eighteen-minute gap –

NIXON (*interrupts*): I don't know anything about that.

HAIG (*continues*): . . . You mentioned the 'Bay of Pigs' several times. Sooner or later they're going to want to know what that means. They're going to want to know what was on that gap . . .

NIXON: It's gone. No one will ever find out what's on it.
Haig moves closer and leans down, very low, whispers.

HAIG: They might . . . if there were another . . . recording.
Nixon glances up at him.

HAIG: We both know it's possible. *(then)* I know for a fact it's possible.
Nixon stares up at him.

HAIG: I've spoken to Ford . . . And there's a very strong chance he'll pardon you . . .
Haig hands him a letter of resignation.
INSERT: 'I hereby resign the office of President of the United States.'

HAIG: This is something you will have to do, Mr.

President. I thought you would rather do it now . . .
I'll wait outside.

Haig drifts out as Kissinger comes out of the shadows. Nixon looks down blankly at the sheet of paper in front of him.

KISSINGER: May I say, sir, if you stay now it will paralyze the nation and its foreign policy . . .
Nixon looks up at Kissinger. The Judas himself – at least one of them. There is irony here that is apparent to Nixon but not Kissinger.

NIXON: Yes, you always had a good sense of timing, Henry. When to give and when to take. How do you think Mao, Brezhnev will react? *(sitting up, suddenly intense)* Do you think this is how they'll remember me, Henry, after all the great things you and I did together? As some kind of . . . of . . . crooks?

KISSINGER *(prepared response)*: They will understand, sir. To be undone by a third-rate burglary is a fate of biblical proportions. History will treat you far more kindly than your contemporaries.

NIXON: That depends who writes the history books. I'm not a quitter . . . but I'm not stupid either . . . A trial would kill me – that's what they want. *(with some satisfaction)* But they won't get it.
He signs the resignation paper. A pause. It lies there.

KISSINGER *(grandiosely)*: If they harass you, I, too, will resign. And I will tell the world why.

NIXON: Don't be stupid. The world needs you, Henry;

you always saw the big picture. You were my equal in many ways. *(then)* You're the only friend I've got, Henry . . .

KISSINGER: You have many friends . . . and admirers . . .

NIXON: Do you ever pray? You know . . . believe in a Supreme Being?

KISSINGER: Uh . . . not really. You mean on my knees?

NIXON: Yes. My mother used to pray . . . a lot. It's been a long time since I really prayed. *(a little lost)* Let's pray, Henry; let's pray a little.
As Nixon gets down on his knees, Kissinger perspires freely. He clumsily follows the President down to the floor.

NIXON: . . . Uh, I hope this doesn't embarrass you.

KISSINGER: Not at all. This is not going to leak, is it?

NIXON *(looks at Henry)*: Don't be too proud; never be too proud to go on your knees before God.
He prays silently, then suddenly, he sobs.

NIXON: Dear God! Dear God, how can a country come apart like this! What have I done wrong . . .?
Kissinger is experiencing pure dread, his shirt soaked with sweat. He opens his eyes and peeks at Nixon.

NIXON: . . . I opened China. I made peace with Russia. I ended the war. I tried to do what's right! Why . . . why do they hate me so!
A silence. Nixon wraps his arms across his chest and

rocks back and forth in an upright fetal position.
Kissinger, looking very distressed, reaches over and
touches the President, trying awkwardly to console
him.

NIXON (*woozily at his hands*): It's unbelievable, it's
insane . . .
On that note, we:
CUT TO:

125. EXT. THE WHITE HOUSE. CORRIDORS AND ENTRY.
NIGHT (1974).
A solitary SENTINEL – a Marine Guard – stands at
strict attention, eyes forward, as we hear the VOICES of:
    The THREE SILHOUETTES of NIXON, KISSINGER,
and HAIG *walking out. HIGH ANGLES allow us to hear*
their VOICES echoing off the empty rooms, and
sometimes catch a glimpse of a passing face. From the
voice we can tell that Nixon has resumed his customary
bluffness, a sense of bravado in the face of defeat.

NIXON (*off*): . . . they smelled the blood on me this time,
Al. I got soft. You know . . . that rusty, metallic
smell . . .

HAIG (*off*): I know it well, sir.

NIXON (*off*): It came over from Vietnam, you know.

HAIG (*off*): Sir?

NIXON (*off*): That smell. I mean, everybody suffered so
much, their sons killed. They need to sacrifice

something, y'know, appease the gods of war – Mars, Jupiter. I am that blood, General. I am that sacrifice, in the highest place of all . . . All leaders must finally be sacrificed.

They turn a corner, come into more light.

NIXON: Things won't be the same after this. I played by the rules, but the rules changed right in the middle of the game . . . There's no respect for American institutions anymore. People are cynical, the press – God, the press – is out of control, people spit on soldiers, government secrets mean nothing . . .

Nixon separates from Haig and Kissinger who bid him a last 'Mr. President.'

NIXON (*remote*): I pity the next guy who sits here . . . Goodnight, gentlemen . . .

Haig and Kissinger depart.

Nixon shuffles back, alone, coming to a stop in front of a larger-than-life, full-length oil portrait of JOHN F. KENNEDY. Nixon studies the portrait, pads closer. Looks up.

NIXON: When they look at you, they see what they want to be. (*then*) When they look at me, they see what they are . . .

PAT, overhearing, comes from the shadows in a nightgown. She looks weary, crazed.

PAT: Dick, please don't . . .

He half turns to her. He is unshaven, eyes red-rimmed, a wounded animal who can no longer defend himself.

NIXON: I can't . . . I just don't have the strength
anymore . . .
*His voice trails off. For a moment, it looks like he's
going to collapse. Pat moves towards him to support
him.*

PAT: It'll be over soon.

NIXON: No . . . it's going to start now . . . *(looks into
her eyes)* If I could just . . . If I could just . . . sleep.

PAT: There'll be time for that . . .
He's barely aware of her.

NIXON: Once . . . when I was sick, as a boy . . . my
mother gave me this stuff . . . made me swallow it . . .
it made me throw up. All over her . . . I wish I could
do that now . . .
Pat puts her arm around him.

NIXON: I'm afraid, Buddy . . . There's darkness out
there.
*Pat is crying now. She tries to soothe him, strokes
his brow like a sick child.*

NIXON: I could always see where I was going. But it's
dark out there. God, I've always been afraid of the
dark . . . Buddy . . .
*Nixon breaks down. She slowly leads him up the
grand staircase – into the shadows of history.*

126. INT. THE WHITE HOUSE. EAST ROOM. DAY.
The EPILOGUE and END CREDITS run over NIXON as

*he addresses the assembled WHITE HOUSE STAFF. PAT
and the FAMILY flank him.*

NIXON: . . . I remember my old man. I think they
would've called him a little man, common man. He
didn't consider himself that way. He was a streetcar
motorman first, and then he was a farmer, and then
he had a lemon ranch. It was the poorest lemon
ranch in California, I assure you. He sold it before
they found oil on it.
*IMAGES of FRANK and HANNAH NIXON now
arise in Nixon's consciousness — a past he could
never really connect his own life to. As if it were a
storybook, a fabled America that never was. The
MUSIC should, in a sense, accentuate this divorce of
sentiment from reality.*

NIXON (*cont'd*): . . . and then he was a grocer. But he was
a great man because he did his job, and every job
counts up to the hilt, regardless of what happens . . .
Nobody will ever write a book, probably, about my
mother. Well, I guess all of you would say this about
your mother: my mother was a saint. And I think of
her, two boys dying of tuberculosis and seeing each of
them die, and when they died . . . Yes, she will have
no books written about her. But she was a saint . . .
But now, however, we look to the future.
*Nixon is holding himself together by sheer force of
will. Many members of his STAFF are weeping. He
pulls an old well-leafed book open, puts a set of
eyeglasses on to read from it, the first time he's ever
worn them in public.*

NIXON (*contd*): I remember something Theodore Roosevelt wrote when his first wife died. He was still a young man, in his twenties, and this was in his diary – 'T.R.' – . . . 'She was beautiful in face and form and lovelier still in spirit . . . When she had just become a mother, when her life seemed to be just begun, and when the years seemed so bright before her, then by a strange and terrible fate death came to her. And when my heart's dearest died, the light went from my life forever. . .' That was 'T.R.' in his twenties. He thought the light had gone from his life forever.

He puts down the book, nearly cracking.

NIXON: . . . But of course he went on, to become president, sometimes right, sometimes wrong, always in the arena, always vital . . . We sometimes think, when things happen that don't go the right way, we think that when someone dear to us dies, when we lose an election, when we suffer a defeat, that all is ended . . . but that's not true. It is only a beginning, always; because the greatness comes not when things always go good for you, but the greatness comes, and you're really tested, when you take some knocks, some disappointments, when sadness comes . . . Because only if you have been in the deepest valley can you ever know how magnificent it is to be on the highest mountain . . . To have served in this office is to have felt a very personal sense of kinship with each and every American. In leaving it, I do

so with this prayer: May God's grace be with you
in all the days ahead.

127. EXT. THE WHITE HOUSE. DAY.
*A MARINE CORPS HELICOPTER waits at the end of
a red carpet.* NIXON *and* PAT *make their way towards it,
followed by the* FAMILY.

NIXON (*V.O. cont'd*): . . . Remember: always give your
best, never get discouraged, never be petty. Always
remember: Others may hate you, but those who hate
you don't win unless you hate them . . . and then
you destroy yourself.
*They climb the steps and Nixon turns on the top
step and smiles bravely. Then he waves good-bye.*

NIXON (*V.O. cont'd*): . . . Only then will you find what
we Quakers call 'peace at the center.' *Au revoir –*
we'll see you again!
*He raises his arms in his characteristic twin-V salute.
And we FADE OUT.
EPILOGUE runs over a DARK SCREEN.*

EPILOGUE: Nixon always maintained that if he had not
been driven from office, the North Vietnamese would
not have overwhelmed the South in 1975. In a
sideshow, Cambodian society was destroyed and
mass genocide resulted. In his absence, Russia and
the United States returned to a decade of high-budget
military expansion and near-war. Nixon, who was
pardoned by President Ford, lived to write six books

and travel the world as an elder statesmen. He was buried and honored by five Presidents on April 26, 1994, less than a year after Pat Nixon died.

We include a DOCUMENTARY CLIP of his FUNERAL, eulogized by President CLINTON, the four other PRESIDENTS alongside him. ROBERT DOLE eulogizes him as a 'great American.'

EPILOGUE (*cont'd*): For the remainder of his life, Nixon fought successfully to protect his tapes. The National Archives spent fourteen years indexing and cataloguing them. Out of four thousand hours, only sixty hours have been made public.

We end on an IMAGE OF YORBA LINDA, CALIFORNIA . . . turn of the twentieth century where it began. We focus on the faces of the early pioneers who settled the land — we drift over the faces of HANNAH and FRANK, in their stern postures — past the BROTHERS, including the two deceased ones . . . to little RICHARD, eyes all aglow with the hopes of the new century.

THE END